Principles
of
Interpretation

Principles
of
Interpretation

STEVEN T. LEVY, M.D.

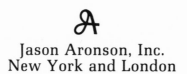

Jason Aronson, Inc.
New York and London

Library of Congress Cataloging in Publication Data

Levy, Steven T.
   Principles of interpretation.

   Bibliography: p. 207
   Includes index.
   1. Psychoanalytic interpretation I. Title.
RC489.I57L48 1984   616.89'17   84-2808
ISBN 0-87668-705-2

Manufactured in the United States of America

To Carol

Contents

7

8

9

Preface

The impetus for writing this book comes from my experience in teaching the theory and technique of psychoanalytic psychotherapy to psychiatrists, psychiatric residents, and other mental health professionals. During individual and group case supervision, seminars, and continuous case conferences, I have regularly observed the great difficulty that psychiatric residents, other trainees, and even relatively experienced therapists have in formulating and making interpretations to patients.

During psychiatric and psychoanalytic training, great emphasis is placed on developing an understanding of normal and pathological mental functioning. Students also learn what is expected to occur during treatment and that their main role as therapists is to interpret what they come to understand about patients in the course of listening to them talk about their lives and their problems. With growing experience, therapists become more comfortable in their role as listener and gradually begin to understand their patients' difficulties in terms of those conflicts of aims, interests, fears, and restraints with which all people struggle, some more successfully than others, depending upon their natural endowments and, especially, their formative experience within their families.

There is a large literature to which therapists can turn for help in understanding the people who come to them for treatment. Students have reported to me with great regularity that even after understanding something about their patients' problems and recognizing how these problems influence the way the treatment is proceeding, they remain uncertain about what to say to patients. It is in this area that the literature is found to be less useful, due to the relative absence of detailed information about what to say, how to interpret, and which words to use and why. Therapists often feel their interpretations are clumsy, unclear, and poorly timed and do not lead the patient in the desired direction. Although all books about therapy, and there are many such books, offer some examples and suggestions about interpretation, a systematic introduction to interpretation as a therapeutic skill is needed. It is this need to which this work is addressed.

There are many reason why interpretation as a technical therapeutic skill to be learned has remained part of the "art" of treatment, a skill that, it is hoped, "comes with experience" or is learned during supervision by more experienced colleagues and teachers. Yet, in most supervision there is too little emphasis on a systematic exploration of principles of interpretation, which should determine what is said and how. Supervisors frequently feel that telling a student how to word an interpretation will lead to a parrotlike repetition of a response, rather than a more natural expression of the therapist's own thoughts. It is true that supervision, despite its helpfulness, is somewhat of an intrusion and a distorting influence upon the therapy, which interferes with the natural unfolding of the therapeutic process. Furthermore, therapists often do model themselves, at least for a time, upon influential teachers, supervisors, and their own therapists as part of the process of internalizing a very special mode of listening to, thinking about, and speaking to people asking for help. However, I have repeatedly observed that even the most serious, dedicated, and talented students, in the absence of direct instruction on how to interpret, resort to a very unnatural, cliché ridden, and often counterproductive mode of interpretation. This seems to be based upon what is actually a caricature of the relatively silent, detached analytic therapist. Observations come to sound like accusations or demands for confession, often superficially camouflaged by such awkward introductions as "it seems to me that" or "perhaps this can best be understood as." Such unnatural and stilted preambles to interpretations, although widespread and somehow communicated from generation to generation of therapists, frequently reflect conflicts in therapists about their own sadism, experienced as a fear of hurting patients with words, and guilt, over seeing and knowing too much that is forbidden. Their unconscious purpose in employing these preambles is to magically modify, via pseudouncertainty, speculativeness, and tentativeness, that which is felt to be too hurtful or too knowing. In another vein, therapists who feel insecure about structuring and timing interpretations, and who are dissatisfied with what they do say, often come to believe their awkwardness must reflect countertransference influences on their work and thus elect to be silent when they ought not to be. This is one of many instances in which lack of adequate training and knowledge is mistakenly attributed to countertransference difficulties.

Emphasizing the importance of developing interpretive technique in the student is not meant to imply that the need for understanding the many unconscious influences that interfere with the therapist's work with patients is obviated. Learning what to say cannot correct defects in empathic and intuitive capacities or resolve the conflicts that distort what the therapist hears and says. Nor can it make up for other

areas of deficient training and experience. To think otherwise is to underestimate the complexity and difficulty of the
therapist's task. However, by stressing clear and systematic
principles of interpretation, problems that interfere with the
process of interpretation come into sharper focus and are
thus made more available for study and correction.

This book will present important principles for interpretation, with special attention to developing a mode of interpretation that optimally expresses the therapist's intent and
understanding, that the patient can best use at a particular
point in the treatment, and that furthers the therapeutic
work. The book is primarily directed at therapists-in-training
and their teachers as a vehicle for acquiring and discussing
therapeutic technique. Although psychoanalytic psychotherapy will be the treatment model addressed, since this is most
frequently the approach around which psychiatric trainees
begin to develop psychotherapeutic skills, I believe the
principles and working hypotheses developed here apply to
all analytically derived treatments and to psychoanalysis
proper.

In writing this book, I have tried to keep it as short and
concise as possible, while allowing room for the development of my ideas and for the presentation of clinical vignettes
to illustrate key points. Because focusing on technical aspects of interpretation isolates certain themes and principles
from many other areas of therapeutic and theoretical knowledge, no effort will be made to trace, in a scholarly and
exhaustive manner, the origin of the ideas presented. To do
so would burden the book beyond its purpose and hinder its
usefulness as a teaching instrument.

Annotated suggested readings appear at the end of each
chapter to broaden the reader's knowledge about specific
points explored in the text, rather than to document fully
the origin of the ideas. These readings obviously express
my own preferences and biases and represent both standard
and classical contributions and, where useful, more controversial, thought provoking, or alternative viewpoints. As

will quickly be apparent, psychoanalytic theory and technique are the backbone of the principles outlined here, consistent with my belief that psychoanalytic theory is the best available "basic science" upon which therapists can build their knowledge and skill.

Acknowledgments

This book has involved many people who gave generously of their time and thought and who deserve recognition and thanks. First, I wish to thank my secretary, Renee Gilbert, for her many contributions to the organization and preparation of the manuscript. Besides spending long hours reading, typing, editing, and revising the text, she has protected my time, tolerated my moods, and been a steadying and encouraging force when I have wanted to run amok. Thanks also go to Bruce Whittier and Bettie Higginbotham for their help in preparing the several versions of the manuscript.

Working on this project has required the relinquishing of many clinical and administrative responsibilities. Dr. Dewitt Alfred, Chief of Psychiatry at Grady Memorial Hospital, and Dr. Bernard Holland, former Chairman of the Department of Psychiatry at Emory University School of Medicine, have, in ways mysterious to me, seen to it that I have had the time and freedom to complete the book. Their support has been much appreciated. Credit should also be given to Jason

Aronson, M.D., my publisher, for his enthusiastic encouragement and continued interest in my work.

The ideas presented here reflect my training as a psychiatrist and psychoanalyst. It is difficult for me to trace specifically who taught me what. In any event, I consider the ideas presented to be my own and assume responsibility for any criticisms of them. Several teachers have contributed to my knowledge of therapeutic technique. At Yale University, Theodore Lidz, M.D., Ruth Lidz, M.D., and Roy Schafer, Ph.D., come immediately to mind as having helped me to formulate those questions around which my knowledge of how to treat people has grown. From the Columbia University Center for Psychoanalytic Treatment and Research, Stuart Asch, M.D., Ralph Roughton, M.D., Burness Moore, M.D., and H. Lee Hall, M.D., in particular, have contributed in many ways to my knowledge of psychoanalysis. At Emory University, I especially want to thank C. D. Tait, M.D., who for many years taught seminars on therapeutic technique with me and helped to refine and clarify my ideas. The many medical students and psychiatry residents who have asked questions about the issues discussed in the book deserve my thanks as well.

Last, I want to thank my wife, Carol Bussey Levy, for her innumerable contributions to the writing of the book. My life and work is immeasurably enriched by her.

Introduction

The recounting of an individual's personal life experience in a psychotherapeutic setting takes many forms. It is the province of psychotherapy to attend to those aspects of the therapeutic process that reveal important information about the patient, but that are disguised and indirect and, to some degree, unknown to the patient. The therapist gradually comes to understand the patient both by listening to him talk about himself and by observing how he forms a relationship with the therapist over time. He is able to view the patient's life and problems in a way that differs from the patient's view because he is more distant from, and thus less affected by, the internal and external forces that have resulted in the patient's difficulties. He must communicate to the patient that which he comes to understand to allow the patient to see himself in a less distorted, frightened, ashamed, guilty, or hopeless way. A new balance will be established, which allows the patient greater freedom of choice and, it is hoped, more satisfaction and less suffering.

The therapist, by way of his greater objectivity, his expertise in understanding people, and his clinical experience in helping others, can come to understand about the patient the things he believes will help the patient develop a more open, honest, and complete picture of himself. These revelations are communicated to the patient as interpretations, involving observations, explanations, hypotheses, and reconstructions, and how they take shape and are communicated is the central theme of this book.

In all the psychoanalytically derived psychotherapies, and psychoanalysis proper, interpretation is presumed to be the central activity of the therapist. Other aspects of the treatment are organized to maximize the effectiveness of interpretations. The therapist creates a setting in which the patient feels safe and comfortable enough to reveal as honestly and completely as possible the painful parts of his life he usually keeps hidden from others and often from himself as well. The therapist seeks to avoid, as much as possible, the intrusion of his own personality traits, values, and outside life into the therapeutic process so that the patient's impact on the treatment, with the distortions that reflect the patient's difficulties in life, can best be studied, understood, and used to help the patient. The therapist must be a steady, nonjudgmental, reliable, and understanding fellow human being who can tolerate the patient's sometimes unrealistic expectations and childish behavior; the therapist must also be available as the patient attempts to fashion a more mature, less pathological relationship. Whenever any activity of the therapist, other than interpretation, dominates the treatment for any period of time, the therapeutic process is not functioning adequately and the reasons for the problem should be explored.

Throughout the book, psychoanalytic psychotherapy will be used as the treatment modality around which the principles of interpretation will be developed, since it is most commonly the basic therapeutic technique taught in psychiatric, as well as in many other related mental health training programs. Patients are seen one or more times a week in a face-to-face verbal interchange. Sessions are 45 to 50 minutes long, with their formal structural boundaries (i.e., time, place, fee, confidentiality) strictly adhered to. Treatment may or may not be limited in time, varying from several months to years. Patients who come for such treatment have emotional difficulties that they, by and large, recognize as psychologically determined and for which they seek relief. Most non-organically caused psychiatric conditions benefit from such treatment. Many patients who seek analytic psychotherapy ideally could benefit most from psychoanalysis, but because of financial, motivational, or other limitations, they elect briefer or less intense therapy. This does not imply that such psychotherapy calls for less discipline, intuitive and empathic skills, self-understanding, and theoretical and technical soundness. In fact, it is most regrettable that almost anyone can call himself a psychotherapist. A certain antitheoretical and antitechnical bias has developed around psychotherapy, in the mistaken belief that experiential and humanistic emphases allow for a better understanding of the patient and maximize the therapeutic benefit of the treatment. In my experience, the lack of theoretical and technical expertise, especially in when, why, and how to interpret, often leads to the subtle erosion of confidence in oneself as a therapist and to pessimism about the efficacy of therapy. Eventually it leads to a failure to recognize the need for the rigorous discipline, restraint, self-observation, and continuing education the patient, often a poorly informed, desperate, and impulsive consumer of mental health services, deserves if he is to be helped and kept from harm. Make no mistake about it, psychotherapy can be a powerful instrument that, when misused, can have a destructive impact by affecting patients negatively, as well as by depriving patients of more helpful interventions.

Throughout the book, a broad definition of interpretation is used so that a wide range of interventions can be discussed. Although all that the therapist says to the patient is not interpretative, most therapeutic interventions should be related directly or indirectly to the interpretative process.

Comments about the setting, explanations, or instructions (i.e., about free association or dream exploration) and questions about historical information all relate to material that is integral to the work of interpretation. Interpretation, defined more narrowly, is the verbal expression of what is understood about the patient and his problems. To the extent that all aspects of the therapeutic process are a vehicle for such understanding, it is legitimate to explore the therapist's comments about the therapeutic process within the broad context of interpretation. Furthermore, to the degree the therapist exercises care and thoughtfulness in his interventions, he facilitates the therapeutic process and maximizes the impact of those interpretations, in the narrower sense, that help the patient understand his unconscious mental life. What the therapist says to the patient comes to define a way of thinking about things together, establishes a mode of communication between them, and determines, to a large extent, what form the patient's new self-knowledge will take. In fact, it can be said that the patient and therapist together interpret the patient's inner and often hidden mental life, in that the patient often amends, corrects, and amplifies on what the therapist says. These interpretations represent what the two collaborators in the therapeutic process come to know and understand about the patient. They are, nonetheless, heavily influenced by the therapist's way of thinking and his manner of expressing his interpretative remarks.

In discussing the principles of interpretation, key aspects of the psychotherapeutic process will be highlighted. These include phases of treatment (i.e., beginning and terminating the treatment), therapeutic interaction (i.e., transference, resistance, the therapeutic alliance), the nature of the material to be understood (i.e., dreams, slips, fantasies), and psychopathology (i.e., character traits, symptoms, acting out). There are certain general rules about how we best communicate to patients, regardless of what we are interpreting. These general rules develop naturally out of more specific interpretations and are discussed in the concluding chapter. Clinical examples with sample interpretations are presented to illustrate the principles of interpretation. They include interpretations made to patients, chosen because they allow important issues to be discussed, not because they are perfect or even the most useful interpretations that might have been made. The reader should then formulate interpretations that are more succinct, clearer, and more expressive of the points being made.

Suggested Readings

Arlow, J. A. (1979). The genesis of interpretation. *Journal of the American Psychoanalytic Association, Suppl.* 27:193–206.

> In this brief paper, Arlow outlines the intrapsychic processes that take place in the therapist that lead to the formulation of interpretations. This is a difficult topic, largely unexplored, to which this paper is a good introduction.

Fromm-Reichmann, F. (1950). *Principles of Intensive Psychotherapy.* Chicago: The University of Chicago Press.

> This book is a widely read introductory text on the technique of psychotherapy. Written from an interpersonal perspective, it provides many useful ideas about how to bring the patient's attitudes and behaviors toward the therapist, particularly negative ones, into the therapeutic dialogue. It also has many valuable suggestions about the treatment of severely disturbed patients, an outgrowth of the author's widely known experiences and expertise in psychotherapeutic work with schizophrenic patients. A wealth of clinical detail helps clarify the technical advice the author gives. Although one could argue with many of the author's theoretical positions, her particular humanity and devotion to the patient comes through in her writing and probably has contributed to this work's appeal to generations of fledgling therapists.

Greenson, R. R. (1967). *The Technique and Practice of Psychoanalysis.* New York: International Universities Press.

> This textbook of psychoanalysis is chosen from among several for inclusion in the selected readings for several reasons. Although directed to psychoanalysts, it is written with an eye toward clear definition of terms, an avoidance of theoretical jargon, and abundant and detailed clinical vignettes to illustrate

key points. Greenson emphasizes the stages in the interpretive process with regard to resistance and transference. He describes confrontation (demonstration), clarification, interpretation, and working through as the four stages of interpreting and gives many examples of each in different clinical instances. He pays considerable attention to the elements of the psychoanalytic situation and to his view of the importance for the working alliance of the analyst's realistic, compassionate, human attitude toward the patient.

Langs, R. (1973 and 1974). *The Technique of Psychoanalytic Psychotherapy, Vols. I and II*. New York: Jason Aronson.

This is the most comprehensive textbook on psychoanalytic psychotherapy available. A clearly written, source book, it provides carefully thought out definitions and explanations of the main elements of the treatment situation and is particularly useful in connection with the rules, boundaries, and technical procedures of psychotherapy.

Loewenstein, R. M. (1951). The problem of interpretation. *Psychoanalytic Quarterly* 20:1-14.

This paper is a very useful general summary of "rules" of interpreting widely accepted within psychoanalysis. It is clearly written, relatively free of unnecessary jargon, and a good introduction to the theory of the interpretive process.

Ornstein, A., and Ornstein, P. H. (1975). On the interpretive process in psychoanalysis. *International Journal of Psychoanalytic Psychotherapy* 4:219-271.

The authors describe the interpretive process from the perspective of Kohutian self-psychology. What is particularly useful in their presentation is their emphasis on the therapist's contributions to the treatment process, the impact of his personality on the patient's response to his interpretations, and the empathic quality of his interpretive and non-interpretive interventions. The authors question the distinctions between interpretive and non-interpretive interventions and advocate a broad definition of interpretation. They examine various restricted definitions of interpretation and conclude that all of the therapist's communications to the patient should be viewed within an interpretive context and usually are by patients.

1

Beginning the Treatment

Evaluation, the Preinterpretive Phase

During early meetings between the therapist and the patient, the therapist's comments consist primarily of questions, explanations, descriptions, and suggestions. The goal is to gather information, make treatment decisions, and launch the treatment process. It is useful to examine these early interventions within the context of interpretive technique because they lay the groundwork for later interpretations, establish a mode and tone of communication or discourse, and if handled properly, lead naturally to the interpretive process without changing the way the therapist talks to the patient or conducts himself.

The therapist introduces himself to the patient and invites the patient into his office. The therapist should call himself what he expects the patient to call him. Especially if the patient is a physician, psychiatrist, or therapist from some other discipline, an ambiguous or informal greeting creates an immediate tension and may mislead the patient about important treatment boundaries. Similarly, the therapist's invitation to begin to reveal something about the patient's life and its problems requires attention to what and how things are said. If the therapist has information about the patient from another source (i.e., a referring clinician), it is important to indicate this to the patient.

> *Therapist:* I have spoken to Dr. A about you. He has told me about your depression, suicide attempt, and subsequent hospitalization. He told me you would be calling me to continue your treatment. I would like you to tell me about these and any other problems you want help with.

There are several points to be made here. Any outside information, that is, facts the patient has not himself told the therapist, must be brought into the treatment. The patient must feel he is in charge of what he reveals about himself and should not have to wonder what his therapist already knows. The therapist's statement should, therefore, summarize what he believes are the relevant points in his extratherapeutic awareness of the patient's problems. If this is not done, patients often feel pressured to "confess" what they imagine an outside source has told the therapist. The therapist's statement indicates the boundaries of the treatment, in that all information about the patient will be kept within the treatment and any outside information brought into the treatment. It tells the patient of the therapist's concern for the patient's predicament, if the patient feels that the therapist already is aware of certain of his secrets and may even have prejudged him. It is a statement of relationship, establishing the patient and the therapist as the unit for knowing things together about the patient. It also affirms the confidentiality of the treatment, disavowing any outside party's involvement in the treatment without the awareness of both participants. In view of all this, therapists should be cautious about obtaining too much information about a patient in advance, although this cannot always be avoided.

In the absence of outside information, the therapist should initiate the patient's giving his first account of his emotional problems. It is often a good idea to provide the patient with some structure in which to present his narrative.

> *Therapist:* We will be meeting for three or four 50-minute sessions in order to hear about the troubles you are having and to make a decision about how to proceed.

This gives the patient an idea about how much time he has and what will happen in the first few sessions. It also is an acknowledgment that the patient is a stranger to the treatment setting. Ushering a frightened stranger into an office and expecting him to know what to do without explanation is a caricature of analytic technique and is never appropriate even if, and especially if, the patient has been in therapy before or is a therapist himself. *Nothing need be or should be assumed*, an attitude that will characterize the therapist's position throughout the treatment.

How the therapist gathers a history is a matter of considerable disagreement, and some flexibility of approach seems warranted. Some clinicians advocate the gathering of a detailed life history with specific inquiry into certain areas (i.e., relations with peers, developmental landmarks, sexual functioning, etc.), in the belief that such information is essential in assessing the patient's difficulties and determining a plan of treatment. Others advocate an unstructured approach, allowing the patient to speak freely about himself, in the belief that the important material will inevitably emerge without structuring questions. Patients differ greatly in their capacity to outline, coherently, their current difficulties and how these difficulties developed. The variables include prior experience in treatment, the degree of the patient's psychological distress, the patient's ease in meeting and talking freely with new people, the patient's understanding of what is wrong, and many other factors that make generalizations about a best approach undesirable. In principle, the therapist should try to help the patient describe his problems in his own way, with as few questions and structuring remarks as possible. This will be the therapist's subsequent approach if a decision to work together is reached, and thus the patient will have some idea of what to expect from the therapist. It will allow the therapist to determine the patient's ability to assume a major, active, talking role in a diadic relationship with a frequently silent, listening, reflective therapist. Many therapists, in the interest of helping patients through the initial discomfort of entering treatment, while also wanting to obtain a complete, detailed history, adopt an outgoing, talkative, encouraging attitude during the evaluation, only to become more silent, austere, and formal in treatment. Although the therapist may be able to justify this, the patient may not understand it. In addition to feeling fooled into choosing to work with the now less friendly therapist, the patient may feel frightened, criticized, or guilty about having done something wrong or angry at the therapist for not continuing to help with questions, comments, and encouragement. This often affects the early work adversely.

A structureless, unquestioning, silent approach gives the patient a different, equally distorting picture of the treatment process. The patient will wonder if the therapist is interested in knowing about him and will wonder if the therapist can make a treatment recommendation, particularly if the patient has not, or feels he has not, given a coherent picture of the problems he seeks help with. This may foster the idea of a therapist who magically knows without being told, who works in strange and unfathomable ways, rather than collaborating with the patient. Although there is much that will remain vague and unclear to the patient about many aspects of treatment, the therapist should not unnecessarily contribute to the mysteriousness of the process.

In summary, a picture of the patient's difficulties, as well as a general overview of the patient's life, both past and present, should be obtained, with the therapist facilitating the patient's self-revelation in a manner consistent with the therapist's subsequent stance, should working together in therapy be agreed upon. Because patients vary greatly in their initial presentation (i.e., crisis situation, referral from another therapist, "shopping" for a therapist), there are no simple approaches or rigid guidelines. The therapist's interventions, level of activity, attention to issues of neutrality, boundaries, confidentiality, and other technical issues should, as much as possible, merge into the treatment phase.

The Treatment Recommendation, the First Interpretation

The therapist's treatment recommendation usually represents the first significant interpretation in the treatment process and, therefore, deserves special attention. The therapist should make a statement that will be a prototype for later interpretations. Because of its special nature, this first interpretation will, of necessity, be longer, more comprehensive, and end in a suggestion or recommendation about what to do. Because there are so many possibilities, a sample recommendation will be given and discussed to highlight the essential elements as they relate to the technique of interpretation.

> The patient, a middle-aged businessman, sought treatment because of difficulties in relationships at work, a marriage he characterized as enslavement to a demanding, complaining wife, and chronic anxiety and insomnia. Throughout the evaluation period, he described instances of his angry submission to the wishes of his colleagues at work, his wife, and as a child, to his distant, authoritarian father and intrusive mother. There was abundant evidence of his hidden provocativeness, his fear of open confrontation, his competitiveness, and his tremendous insecurity and self-defeating behavior.

> *Therapist:* From what you have told me about yourself and
> your problems, the anxiety and troubles in your work and
> home life are serious and require treatment. I think some of
> the problems center around your getting angry and certain
> conflicts that being angry and expressing anger stir up in
> you, some of which remain hidden from your awareness. I
> believe the best way to better understand this and your
> other problems is in therapy designed to help us learn as
> much as possible about your inner life, both things you
> know about and things that we will have to work to un-
> cover by examining your thoughts, feelings, fantasies, and
> dreams in as honest and complete a way as possible.

Several principles of interpretation are seen in this sample
treatment recommendation made in the form of an interpretation. In the first place, we should note the fact that an
interpretation was made. Too frequently, a patient is ushered
into treatment without any interpretative or summary comment by the therapist on what the patient has said during
the evaluation. The patient expects, as he should, some comment from the therapist about his difficulties. Therapists
have many reasons for not responding. Often the therapist
can see so many conflicting trends and areas of psychopathology in the patient that formulating an interpretation
to summarize the problem is difficult. The therapist may
believe the patient is not ready to hear anything about himself so early in the therapeutic process or he may decide an
interpretation will frighten the patient away or induce premature resistance. The therapist may think that an interpretation is unnecessary, that getting the patient started in
treatment is a sufficient indication that the therapist has
heard what the patient has said, recognizes the seriousness
of the problem, and appreciates the need for treatment. Although there is some truth to all this, a recommendation for
treatment without a summary interpretation of what the
therapist thinks about the patient's problems has many
negative consequences. First and foremost, the therapist
introducing an interpretation sets the tone of the treatment
process. The therapist will make explicit, in words, some

area of understanding about the patient, which both therapist and the patient will henceforth include in their working
knowledge of the patient's psychological life, knowledge
that both will seek to expand and understand more fully.
Failure to make such a statement leaves the patient wondering why the therapist is recommending treatment and why
he remains silent about what he thinks is wrong. It also
establishes a precedent for implicitness or assumption as an
important part of treatment. Because assumption, an implicit
rather than an explicit expression, the "unspoken," and other
vagueness about oneself and others characterize psychopathological processes, the treatment should stress openness
and clarity of expression and a shared knowledge developed
through the therapist's interpretations of the hidden, disguised, implicit meanings in what the patient says and does.
Although there are always choices about what to interpret,
it is usually possible to identify a leading theme in the
material, which, as a result of putting it into words, makes it
more available for reflection and further exploration. In the
clinical situation presented, the theme conflict over anger is
presented to the patient as an aspect of the patient's presenting problems the therapist recognizes as centrally important. Inherent in the interpretation, which is of necessity
very general, is the presentation of the difficulty in terms of
conflict, aspects of which need to be uncovered, clarified,
and understood. In this way, the therapist is telling the
patient something about how the therapy will proceed and
what will be worked on. By mentioning the joint examina-
tion of the patient's thoughts, feelings, fantasies, and dreams,
he indicates what material will be used to obtain a new and
enlarged understanding of the patient's conflicts about anger.
The patient is given explicit information about what the
therapist thinks is wrong, that at least part of the problem
can be conceptualized as conflict about feeling and expressing anger. The therapist notes that aspects of the conflict are
hidden from the patient and that uncovering these hidden
aspects by examining the patient's mental life will be central
to the therapy. The emphasis on mutual exploration and

joint understanding includes the patient in the therapeutic activity.

Such an interpretive treatment recommendation goes a long way in allaying some of the patient's fears about the unknown, the mysterious nature of the treatment he is about to undergo, and this relative stranger, the therapist, in whom so much blind trust and desperate hopefulness must be invested. A clear, explicitly stated interpretation does more to allay a suffering patient's anxiety than any reassurance or even emphasis on the importance of getting into treatment with its implicit promise of relief. This last point, an important general principle of interpretation, must be emphasized. Therapists should become accustomed, early in their training, to dealing with their patients' distress, neediness, and demands for immediate help by making interpretations that show the patients something about themselves they can learn from. If therapists can maintain this approach, many types of patients adapt to it in a way that obviates the need for many forms of crisis intervention designed to soothe, calm, support, or structure patients at distressing moments during treatment.

_____ Instructions and Explanations _____

Once a treatment recommendation has been made and the patient agrees to therapy, the structure of the treatment must be established. The patient and therapist should work out an appointment schedule, an appropriate fee, and other particulars. Although discussion of the intricacies of these issues is beyond the scope of this book, a few general comments are in order. The therapist should be as explicit and as clear as possible about the arrangements. This sets the tone for the interpretative interventions that will follow. Nothing need be implicit or assumed, particularly since changes from the initial arrangements and agreements are more difficult to explore and interpret if there is uncertainty about how these arrangements were originally worked out.

Parenthetically, this holds true for the manner in which these arrangements and the boundaries of the treatment are adhered to by the therapist throughout the course of treatment. Only by carefully guarding the regularity and reliability of the boundaries of the treatment situation is it possible to identify and interpret, in a useful way, the patient's contribution to the inevitable distortions of these boundaries. Although the therapist may feel, as well as be, accused of being rigid and inflexible, he is in fact protecting a useful area of investigation and interpretation. Furthermore, in working out the arrangements and boundaries, the patient gets a glimpse of certain of the therapist's conflict resolutions insofar as these arrangements are, in part, for the benefit and convenience of the therapist. The patient's ongoing awareness of the degree of integration and stability of the therapist's conflict resolutions, as they are indirectly seen by the patient at difficult or potentially conflictual moments in the treatment process, beginning with these early arrangements, will reassure him about the safety of revealing his own conflicts to the therapist. This means of assessing the therapist's personality integration is far more reliable, lasting, and reassuring than either statements of reassurance from the therapist or any more general trust the patient may have in the therapist's degrees, professional affiliations, or personal reputation (Langs 1975a,b,c).

After arrangements have been worked out, the therapist helps the patient get started in therapy. It should not be assumed, either that the patient will inevitably figure out what to do, although this may sometimes be true with certain patients, or that therapy will just happen if both participants meet regularly at the appointed hour. There is some disagreement about how and even whether instructions should be given. In keeping with the principles of interpretation, of which these early instructions and explanations are precursors, the patient should have some understanding of how things will proceed. The reasons for this should become clear in the discussion of the clinical examples that follow. In psychoanalysis proper, the analyst instructs the patient on free association. The patient is asked to speak freely about whatever comes to his mind, to avoid censoring, filtering, or changing the form of his thoughts and feelings as they emerge during the session. In psychoanalytically based psychotherapies, this instruction is often omitted, despite the therapist's expectation that the patient will speak freely. I believe that the patient should be asked to speak freely and openly about himself in all analytic therapies and, furthermore, should be told why this is helpful.

> *Therapist:* I would like you, during our meetings together, to speak as openly and honestly as you can about whatever thoughts and feelings come to mind, trying not to leave out anything that seems to you irrelevant, puzzling, embarrassing, or contradictory. Although this is hard to do, teaching yourself to think out loud will give us an opportunity to learn about those aspects of your inner life that, although often not obvious to you, are important in understanding the problems we will be working on.

This sample instruction and explanation, although obviously general in nature and not intended to convey any of the complexities of the free association process, nonetheless tells the patient what to do and why. Thus, the therapist recognizes that the patient, especially at the beginning, knows little about what to expect, is anxious about the strangeness of the therapeutic process, and is eager to get the most out of it by cooperating with the therapist. Furthermore, the patient needs to develop a feeling of safety, comfort, and trust in the therapist, in whom so much hope is invested. The therapist, if he gives no guidance, but rather greets the patient's uncertainty with silence or some interpretive exploration of the patient's difficulty in knowing how to proceed, seriously interferes with the development of a working relationship. The patient has the right to expect some help in getting started, and an explicit statement of what to do and why sets the tone for subsequent explorations of what interferes with the process. To deviate too far from the normal expectation of a person beginning an unknown therapeutic adventure with a therapist, who is presumed to know what to do and what will happen, is to present the patient with a very difficult, unnecessary, and often counterproductive adaptive task. The patient may rationalize the therapist's unexpected behavior as helping the patient take the lead, be assertive, or tell his story in his own way. But regardless of what such rationalizations reveal about the patient's mental life, this failure on the therapist's part to do what is expected, without explaining why, does little to help the patient trust the therapist. "It remains the first aim of the treatment to attach him to it and to the person of the doctor" (Freud 1913), is one of Freud's best descriptions of the relationship that must develop between patient and therapist for the treatment to succeed.

Analogously, other unexpected behavior of the therapist requires an explanation in the interest of helping the patient get started in treatment. For example, not infrequently the patient will question the therapist about his personal life early in treatment.

> *Patient:* I often feel very guilty after yelling at one of my kids. I wonder if that's normal. Do you have children?
> *Therapist:* There will be times during the course of our work together when questions about me will occur to you, which I will not answer. Rather, I will ask that we try to understand the meaning of and reasons for the question. Although my not answering may, at times, be frustrating, I believe exploring and understanding such questions will be more helpful to you in the long run. You were telling me about guilty feelings that arise in you when you get angry at your kids. Your thoughts then turned to me and whether I have children. What comes to mind about this?

This question, with a sample response, taken from an early therapy session, illustrates a useful way of explaining to the patient an aspect of the therapist's behavior that, in most other settings, would be surprising. The therapist had several options open to him. He might have remained silent. Or he might have responded to the patient's conflict about being angry at the children. Another option might have been to ask the patient why knowing whether he had children was important. There are instances in which each of these responses would be correct. But assuming this was the first such question asked in the treatment, the response given here is most in keeping with the therapeutic needs of the moment and with interpretive principles in general. It should not be assumed that the patient knows that the therapist will not answer such questions, even if previous therapeutic experiences or work as a therapist is part of the patient's background. There is enough that is different, atypical, unexpected, and frightening about therapy without the therapist acting in unexpected ways without explaining why. If the therapist says nothing in response to the question, how is the patient not to feel either that it was a stupid or inappropriate question or that the therapist has some unknowable or unspeakable reason for not answering, with neither being the true reason for not answering? Asking the patient why the question came up, without first explicitly stating why the therapist will not answer such questions, is also an inadequate or suboptimal response. Both the patient and the therapist usually feel some sense of evasiveness in neither answering nor explaining the reason for not answering. It is as though there is some collusion in avoiding the tension of the unanswered question by exploring the meaning or reason for the question. This sense of collusion invariably negates any value such an exploration might have. Therapists, especially those in training who feel they are obeying some very traditional and "classically pure" technical procedure by neither answering nor explaining, often feel uncomfortably withholding, guilty, evasive, or at times mistakenly superior for adhering to a distortion of a bit of analytic abstinence. Feeling that they are being unnecessarily hard, evasive, and unnatural toward the patient should not be viewed as a countertransference response in these instances, although this is frequently how supervisors and therapists themselves view the emergence of such feelings around questions not answered early in the treatment. It should be pointed out that an explanation, such as the one presented, does not preclude further questions or even further tension when subsequent questions are explored rather than answered. The patient's curiosity about the therapist, although it will inevitably be frustrated as part of the therapeutic procedure, should not be frustrated with the idea of making it go away or of giving it a pejorative meaning. Rather, it should become part of the material to be learned from, provided the reason for the frustration has been explained so that neither the patient nor the therapist continues to feel in the dark or surprised about the way the frustration was handled. It is worth noting that not only personal questions, but also other questions—for example, requests for the therapist's opinion or advice about something—should be similarly handled early in the treatment. Usually after two or three questions, the patient will begin to examine the questions himself as they occur to him during his free associations. If this is not the case, the therapist, having been explicit about his response to questions, will feel more comfortable in examining why the patient is having difficulty with this aspect of the therapeutic interaction.

These examples of instructions and explanations can serve as models for the many possible instances early in treatment when the therapist should help the patient use the therapeutic interaction optimally. In advocating a somewhat educative approach early in the treatment, I am not suggesting lecturing the patient about how the treatment will proceed or assuming an authoritarian or pedantic manner. Rather, I am emphasizing that the patient's feeling of safety, and of trust in the therapist, is seriously compromised by any behavior by the therapist that departs too far from what one human being new to a process would expect from another held to be an expert in that process. Without such a feeling of safety and developing trust in the therapist, no therapeutic benefit can be derived, and in fact, the patient may leave treatment. In my experience, many therapists, early in their careers, have trouble getting and keeping people in treatment because of their overly frustrating, unnecessarily mysterious manner. In this regard, note that the nature of the therapist's relative silence, anonymity, and neutrality is often misunderstood. The therapist, trying to keep in the background, seeks to avoid injecting his own values, judgments, and personal idiosyncrasies. This helps reveal the patient's thoughts, feelings, and fantasies about the therapist, as well as the distortions the patient brings to all important intimate relationships. These distortions are more easily studied and interpreted if the personality of the therapist remains somewhat in the background. However, in a point discussed by Stone (1961) in his illuminating monograph, *The Psychoanalytic Situation*, these distortions of the "neutral" therapist are most clear and most representative of the patient's typical and therefore most important distortions of others in his life if the therapist's behavior is not entirely unexpected and totally different from the considerate and friendly attitude the patient has every right to expect. When the therapist's behavior is unexpected, the patient may respond atypically. Thus, to be too severely neutral, silent, and anonymous is not to be neutral at all.

Early Interpretations

As the patient settles into the treatment, thoughts about what, when, and why to interpret become more important to the therapist as he listens attentively to the patient. Many factors that determine interpretative interventions will be explored more extensively in the chapters on specific issues in the treatment. Here, the emphasis is more on general principles of interpretation and their application early in therapy when the therapist divides his attention between two broad areas. First, he listens in order to understand the patient's emotional problems and general psychological make-up. Second, he attends to how well the patient is participating in the therapeutic process. Although this is a somewhat artificial dichotomy, it has a heuristic value here. Patients may differ greatly in both areas. With certain patients, the therapist may, after only a few sessions, have grasped the major areas of conflict in the patient, know how and why these conflicts developed, and be able to predict, in a general way, how they will be resolved in the treatment. Other patients, however, will only confuse and puzzle the therapist. Again, some patients quickly adapt to the therapeutic situation, whereas others find talking freely about themselves, trusting the therapist, and even coming to sessions regularly and promptly extremely difficult. Early interpretations should be directed toward both areas, particularly as difficulties arise.

As the therapist begins to develop a working knowledge of a patient's mental life and particular conflicts, many opportunities for interpretation become evident. Even if the patient is articulate about certain aspects of his emotional problems, his self-knowledge is rarely in a form that optimally allows him to understand more about himself in a way that will lead to useful change. From the beginning, the therapist should interpret areas of conflict as the material unfolds. Interpretations should mention the conflicting trends, be they wishes, fears, prohibitions, feelings. Such early interpretations lead the patient to think in terms of conflict, a way of thinking that cannot be expected to occur spontaneously even among psychologically sophisticated patients. It is important to remember that even when the patient seems to be speaking freely and without difficulty during the first few sessions, the therapist should try to identify major areas of revealed conflict and interpret them. For some reason, many teachers and students of analytic psychotherapy believe that no interpretations need to be made to the patient until significant resistance appears. Thus, some therapists might not say anything to the patient during the first few sessions of analysis or psychotherapy. This is difficult for most patients to understand and does little to encourage the patient to develop a capacity for self-observation and psy-

chologically informed reflection. Moreover, it interferes with
the patient's sense of the treatment as a joint venture with a
listening, clear-thinking, plain-speaking, gradually trusted
expert. In fact, some resistances may be induced by an overly
silent therapist early on. As a general rule, the therapist
should probably never be completely silent during any
therapy session, no matter how smoothly the patient's associations seem to be flowing. But particularly during the
early sessions, the therapist's interpretations of areas of
conflict, of connections between one theme and another, of
similarities between past and present, of trends in relationships all help the patient to begin to think about himself in
new, less distorted, less confused ways, which will help solve
his unresolved problems. Thus the therapist, by example,
acts as a model of how to think about things that is far more
useful in developing an effective working relationship than
is making the first significant interaction in the treatment
proper the patient's inevitable uncomfortable response to
the therapist's seeming nonhelpfulness. Although all this
may seem obvious, many patients have spent three or four
hours pouring out their version of their current and past
miseries to a totally silent therapist. These patients may
eventually, no longer able to contain their curiosity and
irritation, ask, "Why don't you say something?" only to have
the first interpretation they hear sound something like, "So
you find my silence uncomfortable." The therapist should
pay particular attention to resistance that occurs in the
treatment, but interpretations should be made at other times
as well.

Early interpretations should proceed from surface to
depth and should meet the patient slightly beyond the limits
of his own understanding. From surface to depth refers to
interpreting what is conscious or close to consciousness
before interpreting what is deeply repressed—interpreting
what is current and much on the patient's mind before
searching for what is forgotten or only dimly recalled. The
limits of understanding refer to interpreting at a level that
takes into account where the patient's comprehension of a
particular issue ends and only increasing the patient's

knowledge slightly. Put another way, the patient, having made clear certain material to the therapist, should be "on the verge" of discovering the content of the interpretation himself. There are several reasons for these two interrelated and important principles of interpretation. Both consider the importance of knowing what the patient is able to hear and make use of when the interpretation is made. Most interpretations show the patient something about himself that he has avoided seeing for some reason or, more likely, for many reasons. When an interpretation is made, the patient may either continue to avoid knowing the content of the interpretation or will have to, in some way, modify his reasons for not knowing. Thus, an interpretation that is close to the patient's "surface" or conscious knowing meets with less resistance than one that bypasses too many of the patient's obstacles or reasons for not knowing: Interpretations stir up resistance, the intensity of which determine whether or not the interpretation will be accepted and expand the patient's self-knowledge.

Other issues involved in these guiding principles of interpretation are particularly relevant for early interpretations. The therapist's interpretative mode should serve as a model for the patient's growing capacity to think about himself and his problems. If interpretations are too deep, too far ahead of the patient, too surprising in their form or content, they interfere with more than the patient's being able to use the new knowledge they reveal. Then the therapist becomes a sort of wizard, with magical powers. Although patients may, at times, wish for an omnipotent, omniscient magical helper and protector, in the long run, no patient really wants or can lastingly benefit from a wizard–magician therapist. Such a view of the therapist, whether fostered by interpretations that go far beyond the patient's knowledge or by an overly silent therapist who occasionally makes an interpretation that seems to "come out of nowhere," does little to help the patient's identification with the therapist's way of thinking about things and making mental life understandable. Instead, it discourages the belief that insight is achieved with the therapist in a collaborative effort. The therapist should per-

haps err on the "slow, not-too-bright" side, seeming somewhat concrete, repetitive, and simple-minded, a stance many
therapists find difficult because of their own neurotic needs
to be brilliant and special in both their patients' and their
own eyes. Interpretations are always a little painful in that
they reveal something the patient did not know, but might
have known about himself. It does not help the patient accept interpretations that include this "painful" aspect if the
therapist's quickness, or unusual insightfulness, is promi-
nently displayed by the manner in which interpretations are
given. Part of the unhappiness and discouragement most
patients feel, in addition to the personal difficulties caused
by their symptoms and character problems, is due to a sense
of their failure to understand and master their conflicts.
Allowing the patient to feel, as much as possible, that he is
taking an active and, at times, leading role in the exploration
and interpretation of his inner life, increases the patient's
hopefulness and self-esteem in the face of heretofore incomprehensible, unresolvable problems. This hope and self-
esteem, which is part of what carries the patient along in the
treatment, does not develop when interpretations are too
deep or seem too much a product of the therapist's superior
understanding and insightfulness.

The second broad area of early interpretation concerns
the problems the patient appears to be having in being a
patient, in working with the therapist, in free associating.
Although many of these issues will be discussed later, particularly in Chapter 4, some general comments are in order
here. As mentioned, one of the earliest goals in the treatment
is to "attach" the patient to the therapeutic process and to
the therapist. The therapist should therefore pay particular
attention to problems the patient experiences in this area.
For example, he should note embarrassment or mistrustful-
ness in free associating, lateness or other problems in coming
to sessions, requests for advice or opinions from the therapist, complaints about one or another of the therapeutic
boundaries or rules. Although patients vary greatly in their
ease in getting started, when problems do arise early, these
problems should be explored and interpreted rather than

allowed to persist in the belief that they will go away. In this way, the patient is introduced to the idea that both the therapeutic process and the therapeutic relationship are a sort of laboratory for the study of the patient's problems. Implicit in early interpretations of such difficulties is the position that such difficulties are expected, inevitable, accepted, and valuable if understood in relation to other problems. A clinical vignette will illustrate a typical early manifestation of difficulty in adjusting to the therapeutic procedures, and its early interpretation.

> The patient, a 35-year-old scientist, sought treatment because of marital difficulties and worsening ritualistic behavior of long standing that invaded all areas of his life. The patient had an obsessional character structure and chronic obsessive–compulsive symptoms. During the early sessions in his twice-weekly psychoanalytic psychotherapy, he spent most of the sessions detailing the problems in his marriage. He also diligently reported any seemingly inadvertent thought or fantasy that came to mind, often with a preamble reiterating his compliance with the rule of free association. The therapist noticed after a while that the patient would begin to check his watch toward the end of every session, and would come to a stop right as time was up, or sometimes a bit early. During one session, the patient, as usual, fell silent a minute or so before the end of the session, checked his watch, and then said he noticed his time was up, got up, and left the office. The material of the hour, as well as of many previous hours, concerned the patient's feelings of anger about his wife's control and domination of him. The last thing he said prior to looking at his watch and then ending the hour was that he was tired of her backseat driving, continually telling him to slow down, pointing out every stop sign and traffic light to him. He recalled his fantasy of driving particularly fast and recklessly to "scare her to death." At the beginning of the next session, the therapist brought up the patient's manner of ending the previous one.

> _Therapist:_ I have noticed, and wonder if you have, that you are careful to stop a few moments before time is up, and

last session ended the session without any comment from
me that the session was over.
Patient: I just want to be sure not to go overtime. (Silence.)
I also have a dread of being in the middle of something and
your stopping me.
Therapist: Dread?
Patient: I don't know what would be so terrible about it.
But I remember thinking several times, "Better not get into
that now," after checking the time.
Therapist: Last time, you were talking about resenting
your wife's controlling your driving, telling you how fast to
go and when to stop. I think there is a connection between
that and your controlling the end of the hour, which pre-
vents me from slowing you down or stopping you. Could it
be the dread is of getting angry and resenting me as you do
your wife for what you experience as controlling you?
Patient: I don't feel in control at all in here. I try to comply
with your procedures and I don't want to run over. I sound
angry, don't I? I don't mean to be. Besides, you're not like
my wife at all. Yet I'd hate it if you cut me off. . . .

This vignette illustrates a useful way of interpreting the
patient's emerging difficulty in the therapeutic relationship
around the issue of control. The therapist had for some time
been aware of the patient's struggles with control; his compliant obedient efforts to cooperate; his attempts to ward off
his anger; his fear of being cut off; and its many implications,
his dread of the therapist and of the transference. The decision to interpret at this point was based on several factors.
The patient was clearly having trouble free associating at
the end of the hour. Because of the material being presented,
the therapist could demonstrate to the patient a connection
between problems inside and outside the treatment. The
interpretation, although not going too far beyond what the
patient was aware of—namely, the themes of anger, com-
pliance, and control and their interrelationship—called to
the patient's attention the value of observing what happens
in the therapy, of making connections, of isolating areas of
conflict, and of fostering working together. The patient responded by observing his angry tone in the face of his

conscious thought about trying to comply; his fear of negative feelings toward the therapist; and his attempt to control them, to ward them off by being careful not to "run over."

In summary, with regard to the content of the material as it relates to the patient's life and problems, early interpretations should be made to identify important themes and conflicts in which the leading elements are clearly delineated. Connections between themes, between past and present, between one relationship and another, should be emphasized. Such interpretations should not lead the patient too far beyond his current awareness, but rather should strive to include him in further exploration and interpretation. Such early interpretations will engage the patient in the active process of self-understanding and provide model ways of thinking about mental life in terms of conflicts as they are embedded within the matrix of a mental life revealed in the treatment as always continuous, past with present, conscious with unconscious, remembered with forgotten, new relationships with old relationships. When problems arise in the process of therapy (i.e., difficulty free associating, being late to or missing sessions, other early resistance), early interpretations should foster the use of the treatment as a workshop for understanding the patient's problems by drawing parallels; making connections; and indicating trends in the patient's feelings, thoughts, and behavior that are recognizable within and outside the treatment.

Suggested Readings

Breuer, J., and Freud, S. (1895). Studies on Hysteria. *Standard Edition* 2:255–305.

> In this essay, Freud's first detailed description of psychotherapy, he introduces many of the basic issues regarding technique and interpretation. It is worth reading because it is historically significant and because it contains many still useful suggestions about technique. The idea of transference is introduced and this early conceptualization should be contrasted with later ideas about the meaning, centrality, and usefulness of transference.

Freud, S. (1912b). Recommendations to physicians practicing psychoanalysis. *Standard Edition* 12:111–120.

—— (1913). On beginning the treatment. *Standard Edition* 12:
123–144.

> These two papers, from Freud's "Papers on Technique," are a
> good introduction to how Freud understood the technical ele-
> ments of the psychotherapeutic process. They are remarkable in
> that most, if not all, of his suggestions are as valid today as they
> were at the time. They serve as the backdrop for many subsequent
> innovations in technique and are a monument to Freud's crea-
> tivity, deep understanding of the therapeutic relationship, and
> ability to learn and change. It is interesting and instructive to
> compare what he says here to what can be seen of his therapeutic
> technique in the *Studies on Hysteria* (Breuer and Freud 1895).

MacKinnon, R. A., and Michels, R. (1971). *The Psychiatric Interview in Clinical Practice.* Philadelphia: W. B. Saunders Company.

> This textbook is a widely read introduction to interviewing tech-
> nique and to psychodynamic formulations about typical groups
> of psychiatric patients. It is particularly useful in its suggestions
> about interpretive interventions most appropriate for different
> clinical problems and accurately portrays in simple language the
> kinds of interactions the therapist can expect when encountering
> patients with various kinds of pathology.

Stone, L. (1961). *The Psychoanalytic Situation.* New York: International Universities Press, Inc.

> This monograph is a "classic" within psychoanalytic circles and,
> while difficult in some ways due to the author's complicated
> writing style, is worth careful study as a thoughtful exploration
> of the nature of the relationship between analyst or therapist and
> patient. It addresses the issues of the therapist's neutrality,
> anonymity, objectivity and concern for the patient in a manner
> which clarifies many of the distortions of these concepts which
> have led to a caricature of the silent, distant, uninvolved thera-
> pist. This caricature unfortunately has influenced many young
> therapists during their formative therapeutic experiences.

2

The Data for Interpretations

The data for interpretations refers to those sources of information the patient and therapist can draw upon to expand their knowledge of the patient's mental life. This chapter will deal with ways in which such data can be drawn into the interpretive process to maximize their usefulness. Because the therapist will attend to kinds of data that will initially surprise the patient, interpretations that accustom patients to using the many sources of information available will be emphasized. Later discussions will focus more on the content of the data with regard to specific issues in the treatment.

Free Association

All analytically oriented treatments ask that the patient reveal to the therapist those thoughts and feelings that come to mind in as spontaneous and uncensored a manner as

possible. (In Chapter 1, the way in which free association is
introduced and explained to the patient is described, along
with a sample statement the therapist might make to the
patient.) Free association as a technical aspect of the analytic interaction grew out of Freud's gradual recognition that
the unconscious forces that are pivotal in creating and maintaining the patient's emotional difficulties inevitably will be
recognizable in whatever the patient talks about. In fact,
they will determine the nature of the patient's free associations more and more as the treatment proceeds and the
relationship with the therapist deepens. This is in contrast
to Freud's (Breuer and Freud 1895) earlier view that hyp-
nosis, suggestion, pressure, and insistence that the patient
remember certain traumatic experiences were necessary to
understand the patient's difficulties. This departure from a
relatively coercive mode of gathering data recognizes that
the mental forces that create and maintain the patient's
problems are not isolated, repressed memories of traumatic
events. Rather, inadequately resolved conflicts among opposing mental trends, distorted by the events of an individual's development, have a lasting effect on all mental functioning and thus can be expected to influence whatever the
patient says, particularly as the patient tries to suspend his
usual critical watchfulness over what he thinks, feels, and
reports.

The patient's free associations, along with the difficulties
the patient experiences in reporting them to the therapist,
are those data of treatment the patient expects to provide
and usually feels most in control of. The patient soon learns
that following the therapist's instructions to say whatever
comes to mind is very difficult. One of the first important
interpretive tasks of the therapist is to help the patient
recognize and use constructively his problems in free associating. The therapist knows in advance that the patient,
however trusting and compliant, will not be entirely able to
overcome his inhibitions, repressions, and other mental restraints by willpower alone.

Patients must be helped to see that their problems in free
associating offer valuable clues to troublesome aspects of

their internal lives, especially inhibiting and restraining forces that keep certain mental trends (i.e., wishes, fantasies, memories) out of awareness and thus unavailable for modification. Before discussing how to interpret problems in free associating, it should be stressed that although this chapter will focus on introducing the patient to the best ways of utilizing the varied data of treatment—here, free associating and its problems—the free association process should be monitored throughout the course of treatment. In fact, whenever things seem to bog down, the therapist should ask himself whether the patient is continuing to free associate and should explore with the patient any difficulties in this area. Many therapists fail to attend to the continuing integrity of the free association process in later phases of the treatment and thereby miss opportunities to resolve the roadblocks in the treatment that are often best approached in this way.

A typical and important early opportunity to help the patient free associate, and use the problems that arise in trying to do so constructively, occurs when the patient reports what he experiences as an inadvertent or interrupting thought while talking about his consciously determined subject.

> A young woman in treatment was talking about her continuing hostile, yet dependent relationship with her mother, including their many fights. She was noting how guilty and helpless she feels when drawn into these struggles.
>
> *Patient:* While mother was playing her usual hurt, misunderstood self, I could feel that old guilt sweeping over me and my eyes getting teary. Right now, suddenly, I'm going over my checkbook in my head. I guess I don't want to talk about mother, thinking about something as dumb as whether I should get a prettier kind of check, like my sister has, the kind with a picture in the background.
> *Therapist:* Often, labeling a thought as dumb or off the point is a way of disguising from yourself the important meaning of a seemingly inadvertent thought. What about the prettier checks comes to mind?

The therapist had several choices here. He might have accepted the patient's explanation that the "inadvertent" thoughts were inadvertent and merely a way of avoiding more difficult material. In fact, there are many times when it would be appropriate and useful to underline the patient's observation that changing the subject indicates that issues surrounding the fights with her mother were being warded off. The therapist, wishing to foster the patient's self-observation, might say, "So we both see how you would like to get away from talking about certain feelings fighting with your mother stirs up in you." Or the therapist, wishing to help the patient explore her struggles with mother, might ask, "What about feeling guilty and tearing up?" However, particularly in the context of helping the patient free associate, these interventions would have deflected the patient from the problem in free associating illustrated here. The patient did change the subject. But she dismissed what came to mind as without meaning. Such disavowals of associations as unimportant or "dumb" are best interpreted early as attempts to hide or disguise certain mental content they reveal, to undermine the illumination of unconscious mental life made possible by treating all thoughts, feelings, and fantasies uncritically and thus gaining access to their hidden, unconsciously determined meaning. The therapist knows that there are no meaningless associations. The patient needs help in appreciating the continuity and purposefulness of all mental events, recognition of which will eventually prove so useful.

The patient is expected to reveal the content of his thoughts to the therapist by saying out loud whatever comes to mind. In addition to reporting his associations, the patient is expected to think about his problems together with the therapist, to speculate, to compare, to connect, to observe, to formulate, to use his associations constructively in expanding self-awareness. Here is a contradiction that must be dealt with early in the treatment process in a way that fosters both free associating and analytic reflection by the patient. Optimally, the patient should easily shift between the relatively regressive, highly subjective, unstructured flow of associations that facilitates the emergence of previously repressed, primary-process colored material and the more objective, intellectual, secondary-process analyzing functions the patient should develop, particularly by identifying with the therapist's way of thinking about mental life. Problems in making these shifts in modes of thinking need careful and thoughtful attention. First, the therapist must be aware that the patient is presented with a difficult task that is, in fact, genuinely paradoxical. To think critically and yet take an uncritical uncensoring attitude toward one's thoughts is not easy. The patient will inevitably use these contradictory processes for defensive, untherapeutic purposes—becoming objective and thoughtful to avoid free associating —or will pour out "stream of consciousness" associations to avoid thinking about what his associations mean. Interpretations should acknowledge the dual task and the necessary shifts. In this way, the patient is not made to feel he is doing something wrong. Rather, he is helped to eliminate the problems in accomplishing a difficult task.

A patient, early in treatment, was noted by his therapist to respond to each interpretation by spending the remainder of the session thinking, in a somewhat intellectual, objective way, about what the therapist had pointed out. Although the therapist felt the patient was trying to use the interpretation constructively, he also noted that the patient seemed stuck in a particular mode of reflecting, which was very different from a free exploration of his thoughts to provide material for interpretation.

Therapist: As you think about what I said, many thoughts and feelings must come to mind that, although they don't exactly follow up the point I was making, nevertheless may turn out to tell us more about this issue.
Patient: I felt like I should respond to what you said. But I also felt embarrassed, and thought to myself that you must enjoy seeing through people.
Therapist: What comes to mind when you think about seeing through people?

The therapist here helps the patient reestablish free association. Interventions like this one, made early in treatment,
help the patient to shift more easily between two different
modes of therapeutic discourse. The therapist might have
interpreted the patient's getting "stuck" in objective thinking as a defense against revealing his embarrassment and
resentment about the therapist's insightfulness. Yet to some
extent, such an interpretation fails to take into account the
difficulty the patient will inevitably have in alternating
between free associating and reflecting. If, after attempting
to help the patient make transitions in the way suggested,
the patient continues to have the same difficulty, a search
for motives of resistance hidden in this pattern would be
more in order and should govern the therapist's interventions.

> *Therapist:* I have noticed that after I make a comment, you
> frequently stop reporting all your thoughts and feelings
> and focus exclusively on the comment I have made. You
> may be doing this to avoid what you feel when I appear to
> know something about you that catches you off guard.
> What do you notice in yourself when I say something?

In this instance, the therapist calls the patient's attention
to a resistance—thinking or reflecting to avoid certain spontaneously emerging troublesome feelings. It is a matter of
clinical judgment about which approach to take, but the
sequence described above is most in keeping with recognizing the difficulties inherent in the free association process
and fostering its optimal functioning.

In summary, free association is perhaps the central source
of data in the therapeutic process. It is an essential part of
all analytically derived, insight-oriented therapies and should
be carefully monitored by the therapist for indications of
difficulty. Such difficulty is itself a valuable source of information, a fact the patient should be helped to recognize
and become comfortable with. Patients vary tremendously
in their natural affinity for this process. Many patients will

need a great deal of help in establishing free association, yet the effort spent in this direction will pay huge dividends in gaining access to hidden aspects of mental life. Interpretations should acknowledge the difficulties involved, including those that occur in the necessary shifts between free association and more objective analyzing functions. The brief examples given should serve as models for interpretations that help establish the free association process early in treatment.

Interpreting Slips of the Tongue

The slip of the tongue is a special source of psychodynamic information. The term "slip of the tongue" reveals something about its psychological meaning. The word "slip" indicates the conviction that an accidental, rather than purposeful event has taken place. The word "tongue" places the accident outside the mental sphere. Yet almost everyone recognizes both his own slips and especially those of others as revealing important information about hidden wishes, beliefs, and fears, the expression of which has meaning and purpose, even if the slip appears to be unintended. In fact, the term "Freudian slip" has become common parlance, indicating a general recognition and acceptance of the unconsciously determined and meaningful nature of slips. Their occurrence during the course of treatment offers an opportunity for interpretation that is often particularly helpful in developing conviction in patients about the ever present activity of their unconscious mental lives.

The slip of the tongue represents a special kind of compromise among conflicting mental trends. Most obviously, the patient allows himself to say something he ordinarily would not say. He consciously experiences what he has said as an accident. There is usually some gratification of a wish inherent in this bypassing of a restraint or inhibition. It must also be kept in mind that slips only occur occasionally, whereas such wishes are ever present. There is thus reason to think that not only is the slip meaningful, but also that the timing of it is unconsciously determined. When a person in treatment makes a slip during a session, one can assume that the patient wishes to convey something to the therapist that is ready to be explored. Otherwise the slip would not occur. This fact leads to the principle that all slips that occur in treatment should be explored and interpreted. Unlike certain themes that emerge disguised in the patient's free associations, which are better left for exploration at a later stage of treatment, slips indicate a readiness for investigation, which should not be postponed. In fact, patients believe that the therapist's failure to explore slips indicates the unacceptability of their content, in spite of their claims that what they said was "unintended" and "without meaning." A careful study of associations following an ignored slip, or one in which the patient's claim of inadvertence was accepted, reveals resentment, perplexity, increased resistance, and often subsequent attempts to bring the unacceptable material to the therapist's attention again. The slip may be thought of as an unconscious communication about the patient's hidden mental processes as they are revealed in the slip, most of which are obvious and designed to attract the therapist's attention. The patient is forced to own up to the unconscious material he has himself called attention to, and thus the therapist should facilitate its exploration.

Slips make their appearance in treatment in several ways. The patient may report a slip made outside the treatment. In such an instance, the patient has already thought about the slip, and the interpretive work should center around the conflicting forces that resulted in the mental "accident."

> A man in treatment had for several months been having an extramarital affair he had gone to great pains to keep from his wife. The marriage had become painful for both participants, but the patient was unable to bring himself to ask for a divorce. He reported calling his wife by his mistress's name during a quarrel.

Patient: I can't believe I did that after all the trouble I've gone through to hide it. I guess I needed to confess what I've been doing.

Therapist: What did you feel when it happened?

Patient: At first I couldn't believe it. I felt anxious, stunned really. Yet, that didn't last long, which surprised me. My wife was outraged and screaming at me, but I felt detached and wasn't really listening to her. I was thinking about trivia at work.

Therapist: In addition to a wish to confess, your slip was also a way of enraging your wife so that she will push for the divorce you want but are afraid to get.

Patient: Maybe that's why I slept so well last night. You know, I expected I'd be up all night worrying, but I wasn't. Maybe you're right. Maybe I was relieved to finally get things over with.

In this instance, the therapist merely adds to the patient's awareness of unconscious motives behind the slip. When a slip in treatment is recognized by the patient, encouraging the patient to explore what comes to mind is usually all that is required. On other occasions, the patient may make a slip the therapist hears, but the slip escapes the patient's attention. Then the therapist should point out the slip. It is in such instances that overlooking the slip can have a negative effect.

The patient described above, prior to making the slip in which he "mistakenly" called his wife by his lover's name, had for some time hidden his extramarital affair from the therapist. He complained bitterly about his wife, and the therapist had occasionally wondered whether the patient had sought out other partners. During one session the patient was nervously playing with a piece of jewelry he was wearing. The patient sensed the therapist's attention on what he was doing.

Patient: This thing is uncomfortable. I got it at a fair. A bazaar, you know, where they sell handmade things.

Therapist: You got it at a fair.

Patient: I didn't mean to say that. Now I'm embarrassed. It just came out. All right, I guess I'll tell you. I can't believe I said that. I meant to say bazaar. In fact, I had carefully planned to say I got it at a bazaar if anyone noticed it, you know, because it's unusual looking. Someone got it for me. Not someone. This woman I've been seeing.

Therapist: In addition to wanting to keep this a secret, you also wanted to tell me about it, and this was a compromise, a way you could do it, by letting it slip out.

Patient: You think I did that on purpose? I have wanted to talk about it, and I have wondered why I didn't want to tell you.

Here the therapist helps the patient understand his letting something "slip out" as an unconscious mental compromise between conflicting feelings. The patient is led to examine opposing wishes within himself and how a consciously unwanted, yet unconsciously purposeful event can function as a compromise, a useful paradigm for understanding certain other symptoms. The interpretation described the patient's conflicting intentions, helping him to begin to think about what was going on inside him, how he was fighting with himself. This eventually led to the patient's exploring how he unconsciously attributed his own critical judgmental feelings about the affair to the therapist, even in the face of his conscious thought that the therapist would remain neutral and might, in fact, help him with these feelings if he could bring himself to talk about them. Although in this instance it is only conjecture, it is likely that, had the therapist allowed the comment about "a fair" to pass unnoticed, the patient would have unconsciously perceived this as evidence of the therapist's not wanting to know or being critical and unaccepting. In fact, the patient's playing with the jewelry, calling his own and the therapist's attention to it, are further evidence of his readiness to reveal his secret and explore its meaning.

In summary, slips of the tongue are a valuable source of therapeutic data. They represent compromises among conflicting mental trends and should be so interpreted. They are unconsciously purposeful communications that, when they occur in therapy, signal a readiness to explore the material they indirectly reveal; thus they should always be interpreted with this in mind. Failure to explore slips deprives the patient of valuable material about his conflicts and of easily demonstrable information about how the unconscious works. It may also intensify certain fears and resistance about the material the slip is designed to call attention to.

_____ Interpreting Unconscious Derivatives _____

The experienced therapist listens to the patient's free associations in a manner very different from the way the beginning patient hears them. The therapist is comfortable in his knowledge that the patient's associations, which to the patient appear random and spontaneous, are in fact governed by unconscious processes that can be understood by listening for patterns, connections, themes, omissions, and other aspects of the patient's words apart from their overt meaning. These indirect clues about the patient's unconscious mental life are known as unconscious derivatives. The therapist will, by his interpretations, make the patient aware of the latent meanings contained in his words and thoughts. Eventually it is hoped that the patient will himself be able to use his observing skills to understand unconscious forces within himself about which he would otherwise remain unaware.

Great care should be taken in introducing the patient to the latent or hidden meanings of his words. Two common errors are made early in treatment in the interpretation of unconscious material revealed by the patient's free associations. The first is to interpret too early and too often what the therapist sees behind what the patient is saying. During the beginning phases of the therapeutic process, the patient is usually struggling to relax his ordinary critical watchfulness over his words, thoughts, and fantasies as he attempts

to free associate. The patient needs to feel increasingly safe
in saying whatever comes to mind. One of the goals of this
process is to allow previously unconscious material to become available for modification via interpretation. It takes
time and effort for the patient to stop censoring his words.
The therapist interferes with this difficult task if he is perceived by the patient to be constantly reading things into
associations, to be hypervigilant with regard to the patient's
disguised wishes and fantasies. Thus the therapist, although
he should continue to listen carefully for derivative meanings, should only cautiously call to the patient's attention
what his associations might imply regarding unconscious
material. Once the free association process is solidly established, interpretations about latent meanings can be more
frequent, although care should always be taken not to get
too far ahead of the patient's own ability to see the unconscious material hidden in his associations. The use of the
patient's own spontaneous reflections about the latent meanings of his words and thoughts, modeled after the therapist's
occasional interpretations along such lines, can guide the
timing and frequency of interpretations based upon unconscious derivatives. If the patient never begins to scrutinize
his conscious associations for hidden meaning, a search for
elements of resistance is warranted. The same is true if the
patient himself becomes hypervigilant, constantly interrupting the flow of his associations with speculations and observations about their disguised meanings. The balance between a relatively uninhibited reporting of spontaneously
occurring thoughts and feelings and a more objective, self-
observing function has to be reestablished. This often requires that the therapist back off from too frequent interpretations of derivative material.

A second common error in interpreting unconscious derivative material is to do so in a manner that appears to the
patient to devalue the manifest content of his associations.
The therapist ordinarily has far more conviction about the
ubiquitous and pervasive influence of the unconscious on all
mental events than has the patient. It usually takes some

time before the patient joins the therapist in such a view of mental life. Initially, he is skeptical as well as anxious about what his conscious thoughts reveal about his unconscious processes. If the therapist focuses too much or too insistently on the latter at the expense of the former, patients often feel that they are not being listened to. Although there are defensive aspects to this response, some of the defensiveness may be due to poor interpretive technique.

> The patient, a young attorney newly employed by a large law firm, had been told during the previous session that the therapist would be unable to keep an appointment two weeks hence. This was the first session to be canceled by the therapist and the patient said nothing about it. During the subsequent session, the patient began by speaking angrily about his work situation.
>
> *Patient:* They give me all the junk work, stuff nobody else wants. I can't say anything about it because I just got there. I'm supposed to be grateful to those old bastards for letting me join their high-class firm.

The patient continued in this vein for some time. The therapist heard this material as a response to his informing the patient of his missing an upcoming session.

> *Therapist:* What you are really saying is that you are angry at me for not being here next week because you feel you have nothing to say about it.
> *Patient:* I guess I am, although I wasn't thinking about it. (Silence.) I can't think of much right now. (Silence.)

The patient seemed upset, yet unable to say much about either the missed session or his feelings about work. When this was eventually explored, the patient reported he felt rebuffed by the therapist's seeming to dismiss his feelings about being powerless at work. In this example, the therapist correctly perceived the connection between the manifest content of the patient's words, his anger at being powerless at work, and his similar, but unspoken and perhaps unconscious resentment toward the therapist for canceling an appointment. However, the manner in which this was interpreted made it difficult for the patient to use the therapist's comments profitably. The therapist's interpretation reflects a misunderstanding of the relationship between the manifest and latent (unconscious) content of the patient's associations. The patient was not "really" talking about his anger at the therapist. Quite the contrary, he was really full of anger at authority figures at work. One might guess that he was also angry at the therapist, or at least felt similarly powerless in dealing with the therapist's announcing he would not be able to keep an appointment. Furthermore, being angry about his work situation might be an outlet for some of his unconscious resentment toward the therapist, a displacement to a suitable alternative object typical of unconscious processes. In addition, his angry words about having nothing to say at work might be considered an unconscious communication to the therapist about having nothing to say about the missing of a session, a communication correctly perceived by the therapist. Yet the therapist, in his interpretation, dismissed what the patient was feeling about his relationship to more senior people at work, which was indeed very upsetting and difficult for this man to deal with. The patient felt unheard and rebuffed.

The therapist should have made a connection between the work and treatment situations in an interpretation that took into account the patient's conscious feelings about his work and their connection with unspoken feelings about the missed session. Telling a patient what he "really" feels, as in this example, negates the patient's immediate internal experience. It implies that unconscious material is more real than conscious experience, an incorrect understanding of mental life, and also sounds to many patients like the therapist believes he knows more about what the patient feels than the patient does. The therapist might have said something like "telling me about feeling angry and powerless at work may have some connection with similar feelings stirred up in you when I told you I would miss one of our appointments." Or the therapist might have said "I think these feelings about your position at work are very much on your mind right now, in part because of my missing a session and your feeling that here, just as at work, you have nothing to say about it." Both these interpretations comment on the connection between the patient's conscious experience and unspoken and perhaps unconscious feelings about the missed session. The second interpretation further indicates that material about the missed session is causing the patient to think about his anger and powerlessness at work. These sorts of interpretations, especially early in treatment, help a patient to make connections between overt and more hidden aspects of his inner life. Later in treatment, the therapist, having made earlier interpretations such as the two suggested, might be able to say more simply "you are mad at work and at me." The patient would himself fill in his awareness of the displacement and begin to explore its meanings based on his already established understanding of his unconscious processes.

In interpreting latent meanings, displacements, distortions, and other effects of unconscious processes on conscious mental content, it is important to avoid jargon and technical terms that give a didactic feel to interpretations and rob them of their immediacy. Furthermore, such jargon often leads to intellectualization, a means of blunting the emotional impact of what the interpretation was designed to convey. Last, it is often the case that when the therapist resorts to using technical terms it is because he, too, is conflicted and defensive about what he is saying. The jargon becomes a way of objectifying or dehumanizing his intent to avoid its emotional impact on the patient. An inability to interpret an unconscious process without resorting to technical language may also mean a lack of clarity in the therapist's mind about the process in question. Thus, an interpretation such as "you are throwing yourself into this new love affair to avoid recognizing loving feelings toward me that frighten you" is preferable to an intervention such as

"your sudden new love affair is a way of displacing frightening feelings of love you have for me." Similarly, saying "your
exceptional kindness toward your stepfather is the way you
keep any of your anger toward him from emerging because
you dread seeing yourself as an angry, bitter person like
your sister" is a way of interpreting a reaction formation
that avoids technical language and is easy for a patient to
understand. At times, psychologically sophisticated patients
may use jargon, often correctly, even in response to interpretations that carefully avoid it. The therapist should note
this, but need not say anything about it unless it becomes
clear that the patient is using jargon defensively. But the
therapist should, by and large, avoid joining the patient in
relying on such terms. This is especially true in treating
mental health professionals, when the temptation to use
mutually familiar shorthand terms is greatest and when
doing so is most likely to be untherapeutic.

Dreams and Fantasies

During the free association process, most patients will, without any specific prompting from the therapist, mention
something about a dream they had, some fragment they
remember, or perhaps just comment that they seem to be
dreaming more often lately. Most patients recognize that
their dreams are in some way connected with hidden aspects
of themselves, regardless of how they may conceptualize
what they mean by "hidden." Similarly, there is a general
belief that the therapist can discern in dreams information
that the dreamer himself is less aware of. Thus when a
patient introduces dream material, the therapist must recognize that the patient is taking a risk, which although it may
be based upon certain distorted and unnecessary fears, nonetheless indicates a degree of trust and willingness to explore
new material. Taking such a risk requires an encouraging
response from the therapist. Particularly in briefer treatments, there is a belief that dreams are the stuff of protracted
analysis, that their exploration is too time-consuming and

difficult and will divert attention from specific conflictual material associated with the patient's current problems toward which time-limited treatment is aimed. In fact, the therapist who fails to respond in some way to the patient's introduction of dream material is giving the patient a powerful indirect message about the avoidance or unacceptability of unconscious material. One common reason for such an avoidance on the therapist's part, regardless of how it may be justified, is uncertainty about how to handle dream material interpretively. This is especially true early in the careers of therapists, particularly in those who have not had specific instruction in dream interpretation.

This discussion will focus on general principles of interpretive work with dreams. Although a detailed presentation of dream analysis is beyond the scope of this book, certain ways of approaching dream material maximize its usefulness in the interpretive process in both psychotherapy and analysis. Perhaps the first point to be made concerns whether the therapist chooses to mention dreams in his instructions to the patient (see Chapter 1). Some therapists, when they speak of reporting whatever comes to mind, include some comment about dreams being especially useful to examine. Regardless of whether this is done, it is important to respond with interest when dream material is introduced by the patient. Although patients vary considerably with regard to their ability to remember, report, and use dreams in their treatment, this can be traced, in part, to the therapist's interest, encouragement, and technical skill in responding to the patient's early mention of his dreams, in whatever form. A careful review of case material often reveals that a patient's early comment about a dream that is ignored results in no further spontaneous mention of dreams by the patient for some time. Similarly, a patient who might be thought to be a poor user of dream material, if properly encouraged, may learn to make interpretive work on his dreams a major avenue for increased self-understanding and behavior change.

Patients and therapists alike are often intimidated by thinking of dreams as mysteries to be solved or cryptic stories to be deciphered. Freud (1900) introduced psychoanalytic dream interpretation in this way. It is best to consider what the patient says about his dreams as a special kind of free association particularly influenced by and presented in the "language" of the unconscious, characterized by displacements, condensations, symbols, and time, person, place, and other distortion. It is neither necessary nor always accurate to view every dream as the disguised expression of a fulfilled wish. Nor is it always a complete "story." Thus the patient should not be directed to discover "the meaning" of a dream. In a general way, the dream should be a starting point for the patient's associations. The therapist might say, following the report of a dream or dream fragment, "as you think about the dream, what thoughts and feelings come to mind?" Or the therapist might ask a similar question with regard to specific elements or images contained in the reported dream. In this way the dream can lead in many possible directions. At times the patient will spontaneously associate to the dream or offer his ideas about what the dream reveals. It is more valuable to understand what the dream reveals than to piece together a cohesive "meaning" of all the dream elements. Such a task often intimidates therapist and patient alike and inhibits the use of dreams in treatment. Again, dreams may reveal contradictory trends and have "meanings" at different levels and with regard to many different issues. Dream interpretation should never become an intellectual exercise. In fact, it is probably better not to speak of dream interpretation per se, but rather to think of using dream material to facilitate the interpretation of the patient's unconscious mental life. Using dreams in the interpretive process is more important than interpreting the dreams themselves.

Patients are greatly aided in their use of dream material if the therapist can, in his interpretations, link observations or inferences drawn from other sources with information suggested by the dream. For example, "the frightening cruelty in your dream, when compared to the way we have seen how you are overly fair in your evaluations of your employees, gives us a hint about why you are so careful when you are making judgments about people. At some level, you must recognize and worry about this trend toward cruelty in yourself and must always be on guard against it." Such an interpretation helps bring information drawn from dream material in line with other, more familiar sources.

The patient should learn to see his dreams as a reflection of many different trends within himself, some more acceptable to his conscious view of himself than others. Both the manifest content of the dream, the part the dreamer remembers, and the latent content, the hidden or disguised elements in the dream, can be the subject of interpretations. Patients benefit from some instruction or explanation about how to look at and use dreams in treatment. Following the first report of a dream, the therapist might introduce interpretive work on dreams as follows:

> *Therapist:* The dream, as you remember it, can be thought of as a reflection of certain thoughts, feelings, wishes, and fantasies in you, perhaps stirred up by recent experiences of yours, which are represented in the dream in ways that make them either more acceptable to you or so disguised that they are at first unrecognizable. We can learn a great deal about you by understanding what these hidden trends are, as well as by seeing how and why you disguise them.

Such a brief explanatory comment can be very helpful to the neophyte patient. It introduces him to the concepts of latent and manifest content, dream work, and day residue in very simple language. It removes some of the mystery surrounding what is being looked for in dreams and makes the patient a collaborator in the effort, often thereby reducing his anxiety about bringing his dreams into the therapy. Such an explanatory statement, followed by a suggestion that the patient report his associations as he thinks back on the dream, or on some element in the dream, is a good way to begin work on dreams in psychotherapy or in analysis.

Patients often introduce dreams with a preamble of some sort that should be thought of as part of the dream material designed to further disguise the dream's hidden elements. Thus, when the patient reports he remembers only a fragment of a dream, this may be designed to indicate incorrectly that what is remembered is unimportant compared to the forgotten portion of the dream. Or the idea of "fragment" may be part of what the dream conveys. It is thus often useful to call the patient's attention to such preambles and to ask for associations to them. Similarly, the patient's comments immediately following the report of the dream may be useful to explore.

Using dreams to their fullest advantage requires that the patient be encouraged to free associate to dream elements. The patient must be an active collaborator in dream interpretation in order to avoid a sense of speculation and lack of conviction on his part with regard to the therapist's interpretations. Whenever possible, the patient's own ideas should be sought so that he becomes familiar with unconscious mechanisms that are sometimes most clearly seen in dream material.

Fantasies, whether occurring spontaneously during sessions or remembered and reported by the patient, are similar to dreams in revealing important material, although there is usually less distortion and disguise. Again, the patient is taking a chance and should be responded to with interest in and exploration of the fantasy. A spontaneous fantasy involves a temporary suspension of a person's usual watchfulness over what he allows himself to think. Often what emerges is a wishful version of some event the patient cannot allow to happen in real life because of inhibiting forces within him. Therefore, as in the dream, not only the hidden wishes are important, but also the information about how and why these wishes are warded off. In dreams, this information is often discernible in the distortions and disguises that give the dream its fantastic nature. With fantasies, it is often useful to comment on what the patient feels might interfere with such a fantasy coming true. Clues about this are usually to be found in the patient's associations to the elements of the fantasy. In work on dreams and fantasies, the therapist should take care that his interpretations are not exclusively or even primarily directed toward the secret or unacceptable wishes revealed in the dream. To do so often stops patients from bringing up dreams and thus deprives the therapist and patient alike of material that Freud referred to as "the royal road to the unconscious."

The Treatment Setting

The treatment setting includes a set of routines, boundaries, conventions, and rules that are designed to maximize the security, productivity, and therapeutic potential of the treatment. The therapist and, later, the patient as well, monitor and protect the integrity of the treatment setting, recognizing it as an essential ingredient in the therapeutic process. The setting itself, and particularly deviations and disturbances in its boundaries and routines, can become an important source of material for interpretation. The therapist should take care to establish and adhere to a routine in his work that is considerate of the patient's and his own needs for comfort and privacy. As described in Chapter 1, procedures should be explained to the patient in simple language. Once a routine is established, it becomes possible to observe deviations and explore their meaning.

The therapist will observe that the patient gradually adapts to the patterns and routines of the therapeutic process. Because of the ever present influences of unconscious processes, especially those connected with important unconscious conflicts associated with the difficulties for which the patient has sought treatment, it can be expected that these unconscious conflicts will affect the way the patient responds to and inevitably distorts the therapeutic setting— often its boundaries and rules. The therapist should be ever attentive to such distortions, which can then serve as the basis for very valuable interpretive interventions. The therapist's care in providing a stable, reliable, and predictable setting for the treatment will pay handsome dividends in this regard, besides assuring a secure environment for the patient to explore his inner life. An infinite variety of distortions and deviations can arise and serve a useful interpretive purpose, if properly handled. Lateness, problems with the payment of fees, accidental extratherapeutic contacts between the patient and therapist, difficulty beginning or ending sessions, vacations, and scheduling problems are all potential sources of useful data. The therapist should, in general, allow some time for the routines of the setting to become established and familiar to the patient before commenting about deviations. As mentioned earlier, certain aspects of the setting should be explicitly explained to the patient. The therapist's behavior should be predictable and, to a lesser extent, so should that of the patient before setting issues can best be used as material for interpretation. For example, provided that the therapist has been punctual, the patient's first five-minute lateness probably should not be commented on. On the other hand, the patient's repeated lateness is a useful source of material, as is absolute punctuality in certain patients. Interpretations about setting issues made too early, too often, or too aggressively tend to lack conviction, make the patient too self-conscious, and lend an air of hypervigilance to the treatment that interferes with other therapeutic activities. The therapist must make choices about when to intervene. He should listen for general themes in the material and relate these, in his own thinking, to deviations in the setting before beginning to explore with the patient the meaning of the deviations.

> A woman in analysis was working on problems in her sexual life with her husband. Although she enjoyed their sexual activity together, she was troubled about her inability to be sexually aggressive. Her husband always had to take the initiative in their lovemaking. Only if he did so was she able to feel comfortable. The therapist had observed for some time that this patient would always sit on the couch until he sat down in his chair behind her, at which time she would lie down. On one occasion, the therapist

began to sit down, then realized he had left his note pad on a desk across the room. The patient, who had begun to lie down, upon seeing the therapist get up and reach for his note pad, sat bolt upright. Once the therapist sat back down, she again was able to lie down.

The patient began talking about an incident she had mentioned earlier in the analysis, one that involved her mother accusing her of being sexually indiscreet with regard to her father in allowing him to see her taking a bath. The therapist had explored with the patient the meaning of her reluctance to take the lead in her sexual activity, interpreting it as a way of avoiding feeling she was being seductive, a feeling that made her remember her mother's accusations and the incestuous material associated with them.

Therapist: I have noticed, as I'm sure you have, that you always make sure I sit down before you lie down. I think this means that when you are with me, lying down first is taking the sexual lead, stirring up familiar reproaches in you as well as revealing the way our relationship has taken on a sexual meaning.

The patient responded, after an embarrassed silence, that she dreaded the idea of the therapist thinking she was being seductive. This led to many associations about the emerging erotic transference, given sudden immediacy by the therapist's interpretation of what had just happened, triggered by a momentary change in the routine of the therapeutic setting. The therapist's interpretation was in keeping with the material being worked on and occurred after the behavior in question had been well established and, in fact, was accentuated by his getting up to get his note pad. Because setting issues are tangible, their interpretation has great impact, conviction, and often moves the treatment forward in very helpful ways.

In summary, it can be said that material for interpretations is limitless. First and foremost, the patient's spontaneously occurring thoughts and feelings, revealed in as un-

critical a manner as the patient is capable of, are the primary
source of material to be understood. The therapist should
take great care to ensure the integrity of the process of free
association by actively interpreting interferences as they
inevitably develop. Slips, unconscious derivatives, dreams,
fantasies, deviations in the boundaries of the setting, and
many other kinds of data will emerge as the treatment proceeds. They are drawn into the interpretive process by the
linking together of different kinds of data, which are invariably influenced by those unconscious mental processes
that continually impinge upon everything the patient thinks,
feels, and does, and that determine and maintain the patient's
emotional problems. Together the patient and therapist
translate the data into a coherent picture of the patient's
difficulties in the form of interpretations that describe, more
accurately than the patient has ever been able to do, how
and why he has become who he is and what is required for
change to take place.

_____ Suggested Readings _____

Altman, L. L. (1969). *The Dream in Psychoanalysis*. New York:
    International Universities Press.
        This is a useful standard text on psychoanalytic dream inter-
        pretation. Even for the non-analyst, it offers many useful clinical
        examples and outlines both the theory of dream formation and
        dream interpretation in a clear, easily understood manner. Many
        of the suggestions are easily applied to the modified work with
        dreams that takes place in psychotherapy.
Erikson, E. H. (1954). The dream specimen of psychoanalysis.
    Journal of the American Psychoanalytic Association 2:5–56.
        This paper is included because it is worth intensive study in
        connection with dream interpretation. In it, Erikson demonstrates
        the incredible richness of material that can be derived by care-
        fully studying a dream, in this case, the "Irma Dream," which
        Freud used in *The Interpretation of Dreams* (1900) to introduce
        his clinical theory of dream interpretation. Although the depth

and breadth of Erikson's analysis probably goes far beyond what might take place in clinical work, it indicates the many levels of understanding from which a dream may be approached.

Freud, S. (1900). The Interpretation of Dreams. *Standard Edition* 4 and 5:1–625.

This monumental work is included because of its special position in the psychoanalytic and psychiatric literature. Although difficult in places, especially in areas of theory, it is an indispensable source book to which the student should return repeatedly for further understanding about unconscious processes, in general, and about dream interpretation, in particular.

Freud, S. (1901). The Psychopathology of Everyday Life. *Standard Edition* 6:53–105.

Freud's essay on slips of the tongue in this book is a good introduction to the topic of slips and provides a background for discussing the interpretive management of slips as they are reported by patients or occur during psychotherapeutic hours. In fact, this entire book is worth reading because of the clarity of Freud's descriptions of unconscious processes and his explanation of their meaning and interpretation.

Greenson, R. R. (1970). The exceptional position of the dream in psychoanalytic practice. *Psychoanalytic Quarterly* 39:519–549.

This paper argues against neglecting the unique opportunities afforded by dream interpretation for understanding unconscious mental life and helping the patient to change. It stresses the primary importance of using the patient's associations to the elements of the dream in the interpretive process rather than interpreting according to preformed theoretical convictions about mental processes and psychopathology. Greenson also mentions the detrimental effects of avoiding dream interpretation. The numerous clinical vignettes illustrate different interpretive approaches to dreams.

Langs, R. (1975b). The therapeutic relationship and deviations in technique. *International Journal of Psychoanalytic Psychotherapy* 4:106–141.

This important and particularly clear paper examines the structure and boundaries of the therapeutic relationship and its "ground rules" and explores the consequences of deviating from these rules, violating the boundaries, and in other ways threatening the structure of the treatment relationship. Clinical vignettes illustrate patients' incorporative responses to such deviations and their attempts to restore security to the treatment relationship. The author believes that patients carefully monitor the therapist's deviations in technique, particularly around the patient–therapist relationship and its boundaries, as a way of measuring the therapist's mastery over his own intrapsychic conflicts and inner needs. Langs believes most deviations are unnecessary and based on countertransference needs of the therapist. He describes reparative measures to be taken when an unnecessary deviation has occurred.

Langs, R. (1976). *The Bipersonal Field.* New York: Jason Aronson.

In this work, Langs examines, via commentary on several extended case illustrations, the impact of the patient and the therapist on the therapeutic relationship. He particularly emphasizes the way each participant introduces aspects of his own psychopathology into the bipersonal field by variously distorting or deviating from the boundaries or ground rules of the therapeutic setting. Although one might argue about the author's insistent emphasis on the therapist's pathology, his exploration of the importance of the therapeutic setting as a vehicle for dynamic distortion that can become the data for important interpretive work is a valuable contribution.

Loewenstein, R. M. (1956). Some remarks on the role of speech in psychoanalytic technique. *International Journal of Psycho-Analysis* 37:460–468.

This erudite discussion of the role speech plays in various intrapsychic and interpersonal activities affords many useful insights into the dynamic actions of free association, verbalization in general, and interpretations within the therapeutic dialogue. The relation of verbalization to insight and of insight to change are also examined.

Loewenstein, R. M. (1963). Some considerations on free association. *Journal of the American Psychoanalytic Association* 11: 451–473.

This paper describes in detail the dynamic forces involved when the patient is called upon to obey the "fundamental rule" and report uncritically all his associations. Loewenstein also describes the paradox introduced by the interpretive process that asks the patient to understand himself through his associations, a task contradictory to the uncritical reporting of his spontaneously occurring thoughts, feelings, and fantasies. The author further elaborates on his earlier (1956) investigation of the functions of speech within the analytic process, particularly the regressive alteration in the meaning of speech and its discharge functions.

Stolorow, R. D. (1978). Themes in dreams: A brief contribution to therapeutic technique. *International Journal of Psycho-Analysis* 53:473–475.

>   This brief paper is useful in illustrating a way to help patients make use of dream material, in both analysis and psychotherapy. The therapist's identification of an organizing theme in the manifest content of a dream can be a useful place for beginning the associative process in contrast to the usual method of having the patient associate to individual dream elements. A simply described clinical illustration is provided.

3

The Therapeutic Alliance

The therapeutic alliance is a concept that has evolved gradually as psychoanalytic technique has developed and has become part of the parlance of most psychoanalytically derived psychotherapeutic approaches. Freud at different times referred to the "rapport" between patient and therapist, to the non-erotic positive transference, and to the "analytic pact" to describe the cooperative working relationship that develops during treatment. Sterba (1934) emphasized the patient's identification with the analyst's observing and analyzing functions. Zetzel (1956) introduced the term therapeutic alliance to describe this cooperative working relationship and distinguished it from other transference manifestations. Greenson (1965b) refined the relationship of what he called the "working alliance" to other aspects of the interaction between patient and therapist in a way that has proven clinically and conceptually useful.

The therapeutic alliance refers to the ongoing working relationship between patient and therapist as an attempt both to understand and modify those problems for which the patient has sought treatment. It requires respect and co-operation, a mutuality of intention, and recognition and maintenance of therapist and patient role boundaries and is dominated by conscious, secondary-process, reality-oriented interactions. The therapeutic alliance stands in opposition to those elements of the therapeutic relationship reflecting the distortions the patient brings to the work of treatment. These distortions are based primarily on unconsciously determined wishes and fantasies in the patient, many of which play a significant role in the development and main-tenance of the patient's illness. These other elements, deter-mined as they are by unconscious motives, are not rooted in the mutually agreed upon task of working on understanding and modifying the patient's emotional difficulties. Although the therapeutic alliance as a pragmatic construct seems clear, in fact, no such separation of one part of a relationship from another is really complete, given the multiple determinism and continuity of all mental events. Clinically, the thera-peutic alliance has remained a useful way of describing and thinking about certain elements in the treatment relationship that must be present most of the time and must withstand the intrusion of other, less therapeutically motivated aspects of the complicated relationship between patient and thera-pist on the work of treatment.

The therapeutic alliance can be thought of as prerequisite to the patient's using the therapist's interpretations to his best advantage. Therefore, many of the therapist's early interpretations should be designed to foster and solidify the development of the therapeutic alliance. Conceptual clarity on the therapist's part about the elements of the therapeutic alliance helps in formulating these early interventions. The therapist seeks to create a situation in which the patient and the therapist will look together at the patient's life and problems as they emerge during the patient's narrative in the sessions. The patient is asked to experience in an emo-tionally involved and uninhibited way and also to observe and think about himself in a more objective and reflective way, by no means an easy juxtaposition of tasks. The therapist must encourage both trends in the patient by creating an atmosphere of safety for the experiential task and by lending his more objective, experience-distant, psychologically informed approach as a model for and support of the patient's self-observing task. A balance between the experiential and the reflective must be established and continually monitored during the treatment, with the therapist's and the patient's contributions varying with the flow of the therapeutic process.

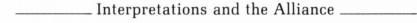

Interpretations and the Alliance

The therapeutic alliance should develop early in the treatment process. It depends on how the therapist takes a history, makes recommendations, and initiates the treatment via his explanations, instructions, and handling of the early sessions. The need for clarity, fairness, and sensitivity to the patient's understandable lack of familiarity and anxiety in these early sessions has already been stressed. Some typical interpretive situations that often occur in therapy will serve to illustrate how the therapist's early interpretations should be directed toward developing and supporting the joint observing and reflecting that is at the heart of the therapeutic alliance.

> The patient is talking about various aspects of his marriage in a relatively free and natural-sounding manner. As he begins to talk about his sexual relations with his wife, his voice drops, he stumbles over his words, and he becomes obviously uncomfortable. The therapist observes the patient's discomfort and wishes to call the patient's attention to the fact that trouble talking about a subject can serve as a clue to underlying conflict about it.
>
> *Therapist:* Are you uncomfortable talking about having sex with your wife?

This intervention, as a question, emphasizes the patient's admitting something to the therapist. Such questions are usually rhetorical, which the patient recognizes, and thus tend to make the patient defensive. Why is the therapist seeming to be uncertain or tentative about what he knows? Patients in this situation often feel that what the therapist appears to know must in some way be bad, if the therapist attempts to make his interpretation tentative or "safer" by turning it into a question.

> *Patient:* No, I don't think so.

This response to the therapist's interpretation as a question makes it difficult for both therapist and patient to proceed. The patient may feel forced to talk "freely" about sex with his wife in order to avoid appearing defensive. The therapist, whose intention it was to examine with the patient the latter's discomfort in speaking of sexual matters, must either insist that the patient really was uncomfortable or more likely wait for another opportunity to explore this issue.

> *Therapist:* You appear to be uncomfortable talking about having sex with your wife.

This interpretation as a statement is preferable to the earlier question. However, in terms of strengthening the development of the therapeutic alliance, it still leaves the therapist as the observer and the patient as the one observed. Furthermore, it may be unclear to the patient why the therapist has made this observation and what direction both should take.

> *Therapist:* Your discomfort in talking just now points us toward conflicting feelings about sex with your wife, which we can uncover and explore together. What comes to mind about this?

This interpretation requires no confession by the patient. It emphasizes the mutual observing function of both therapist and patient, underscored by the use of the pronouns we and us. It aims at the joint exploration of conflict underlying what is observed together, thus giving the patient a direction to follow. Nothing furthers the development of the alliance more than the therapist's helping the patient achieve a relatively comfortable and clear context in which to explore issues that emerge from what he talks about and experiences during his sessions, especially early in the treatment. Seeing that there is a way to view and think about heretofore incomprehensible problems together with another person who is careful not to put the patient on the spot or leave him directionless or in ignorance of the way that person is thinking, helps the patient feel more trusting, confident, and hopeful, all important substructures of the alliance. The interpretation, although very general, underscores the centrality of conflict as a subject of mutual interest in the therapeutic work. As mentioned earlier, patients can best think about their inner life as conflicting feelings, wishes, fears, and other mental trends in relation to their problems, and these conflicts should therefore be highlighted by the therapist in early interpretations. In summary, this interpretation calls attention to observing together the patient's discomfort about sex with his wife, relates the discomfort to conflicting feelings, and invites the patient to explore what comes to mind about these conflicting feelings, indicating a direction in which the patient can continue to reveal more about himself.

> The patient, a depressed woman in her mid-twenties, spent many of her early sessions silent and fearful. When she spoke, she emphasized her conviction that the therapy wasn't helping and that she needed more from the therapist to "get me through" the week. She also spoke of how she felt demanding and unsatisfied in her relationships with her boyfriend, her roommate, and her mother. The therapist frequently felt attacked and believed that the patient neither accepted the interpretations offered nor even seemed able to think very much about what the therapist said. He felt that the patient had created, with the therapist, a situation similar to her other important relationships, namely that nothing anyone gave her was adequate and that she always felt herself to be an unsatisfied, demanding, and therefore unlovable person.

There are many directions a therapist might take in such a situation. This clinical example illustrates an instance in which the patient repeats in the treatment her conflicted relationships with people important to her outside of treatment. The impaired state of the alliance leads to the direction the therapist should take in his interpretive intervention. The therapist felt, among other things, that the patient could not hear or use his comments, could not even think about them. Interpretations require that the therapist is talking to someone who can hear and think about what is said. Although it is inevitable and in fact desirable for the patient's interpersonal distortions to enter into the treatment process, where they can be observed, explored, understood, and it is hoped, modified, a working relationship between patient and therapist must be present in order to examine those distortions. The therapist felt that there was no such working relationship. Thus, the interpretation to be made should be in the service of emphasizing the relative absence of the alliance rather than the dynamics of the patient's dissatisfied and demanding feelings.

> *Therapist:* We don't seem to be at a place where we can think together about these angry, demanding, and unsatisfied feelings that trouble you so. My comments to you seem to stir up the very feelings we can't as yet examine together. What have you noticed in yourself when I say something to you?

This interpretation establishes the alliance as in need of reparative work. The "we" rather than "'you' don't seem to be in a place . . . ," and the reference to thinking "together" point toward the creation of a situation in which patient and therapist are allied in working on the problems the patient presents. By the way the interpretation is structured, the problems to be thought about and the patient's angry, demanding, and unsatisfied feelings are separated from the patient and the therapist who are to think about them. This is in the service of helping the patient to objectify the prob-

lem to be dealt with in order to facilitate observation together with the therapist. The next part of the interpretation
attempts to explain the problem in the alliance, namely that
the interpretations the therapist makes, and by implication,
the relationship itself, have become caught up with the
troublesome feelings the patient reports. The therapist might
have emphasized the relationship, rather than the interpretations, stirring up feelings, but emphasizing the interpretations themselves aids in focusing on what, at this point
in the process, was felt to be more specific and, for the
patient, easier to observe and explore objectively, namely
what she felt when the therapist spoke. The therapist
thought that, had feelings toward himself been stressed, the
patient might possibly have been led either in the direction
of similar feelings toward other important people or toward
feelings about the therapist as yet too diffuse as well as too
intense for the patient to begin to think about in a relatively
objective manner. What the therapist said emphasized the
important role of interpretations and the need for clear
communication around this central and unique aspect of the
therapeutic situation. The last part of the interpretation
again invites the patient to observe herself, specifically
those feelings stirred up in her in response to the therapist's
comments to her. By giving direction to the patient's self-
observing task and by "objectifying" the problem in relative
isolation from everything else going on, the interpretation
will move in the direction of furthering the patient's capacity
for observing, in addition to experiencing. It indicates to the
patient how important the therapist feels being able to think
together about things really is. There is no complaint or
accusation that the patient is being troublesome. Neither is
there any demand that the patient do anything different.
What is offered is an explanation at a level the patient can, it
is to be hoped, hear, stated specifically and objectively, with
a direction for further work.

> *Patient:* You know, I often don't listen when you start
> talking. How screwed up can you get? But then, what good

is talking anyway? We could talk for ten years and I might
not feel any better.
Therapist: From your observation that you don't always
listen, we can surmise that you keep us from both thinking
about the same thing, from working together on a problem.

The therapist's interpretation of one aspect of the patient's
not listening to what the therapist says deserves discussion
because it illustrates several points about interpretive technique. In response to the therapist's earlier comment, the
patient observes that, in fact, she does not always listen
when an interpretation is made. This bit of self-observation,
indicating her recognition of something of value in what the
therapist said, is followed by her seeing something "crazy"
in not listening, some problem in herself. She then retreats
to a more general dismissal of any value in the therapeutic
dialogue; in a sense she backs off from a little bit of thinking
together with the therapist. This response to an interpretation is very common, especially in patients who find establishing a working alliance difficult. The therapist picks up
on the patient's rapid disavowal of the shared thought by
making a second interpretation that reiterates the initial
point, now including the patient's observation, "I often don't
listen," with his own observation about difficulty in thinking
together, stressing the patient's activity in keeping an alliance from developing. It is often useful to repeat interpretations, especially if some response from the patient can be
included to foster working together. Therapists often make
an interpretation and then "drop it" if the patient does not
immediately get to work on the issue at hand. Most interpretations need to be made over and over again throughout
the treatment process, even in the face of the patient sometimes complaining about the repetition or claiming to already
know the point being made. More will be said about this in
the section on working through in Chapter 9, but in this
instance, repeating or elaborating on the patient's observation and integrating it into the second interpretation fosters

the idea of working together, observing together, making joint contributions to what can be known. A second point to be made is that the interpretation stays with the theme raised by the first interpretation, namely a problem in working together. Isolating or emphasizing what the therapist feels is the leading theme helps the patient to develop her ability to think psychologically with the therapist. The therapist might have inquired about what "crazy" meant or pointed out how the patient retreated to a hopeless, "what's the use" position. By choosing to stay with the theme, the therapist felt he had the best chance of helping the patient to examine the problems in working together. Such choices are always difficult and require experience gained from trial and error with each patient. What is important in acquiring interpretive skill is that the underlying principles guiding the choices be explicit in the therapist's thinking so that a working knowledge of the technical aspects of interpreting develops. Also noteworthy is the way the therapist's interpretation highlights the patient's activity or active role in the problems with the alliance. As is repeatedly stressed throughout the book, interpretations should help patients to recognize, accept, and modify their own activity in the creation and maintenance of their difficulties. Because people so often experience their problems as unwanted afflictions over which they have little or no control, an important principle of interpreting is the unmasking of their active, if often hidden participation in their problems. This is accomplished by speaking of mental life in terms of the patient's activity. [In this regard, Schafer's (1976) "action language" as it relates to technique and theory is worth intensive study.] By noting both that the patient had made an observation about herself and that "you keep us from both thinking about the same thing," the therapist stresses, in the former instance, the patient's active participation in the work of treatment and, in the latter instance, her active interference in working together. This way of putting things helps the patient realize that her many conflicting, contradictory activities are at the

heart of her emotional difficulties both within and outside
the therapeutic setting.

The patient, a depressed middle-aged man with obsessional
and masochistic character pathology, entered treatment because of severe marital difficulties and persistent suicidal
ruminations. He quickly established a pattern in his sessions of reporting, in meticulous detail, aspects of both his
unhappy childhood and his self-defeating, day-to-day experiences. There were no silences, and in fact, the therapist
noted that the patient never seemed to stop, even momen-
tarily, to think about anything he had said. Furthermore,
there were few if any opportunities for the therapist to
make a comment without interrupting. When the therapist
did offer an interpretation, the patient winced as though in
pain and at times might say "boy, that hurts" and then
continue detailing his unhappiness. The therapist understood what was occurring as follows: The patient was
obediently following the therapist's instructions to say
whatever came to mind. However, the overly detailed and
interruptionless style of talking, without much room for
thinking or dialogue with the therapist, made the therapist
feel he was being controlled, put off, held at bay. Furthermore, when the therapist was able to interpret something,
the patient seemed injured rather than interested. The
therapist recognized, in the way the patient was dealing
with the treatment situation, aspects of the patient's character pathology, his need to control, to obey, to suffer, to be
alone. The immediate issue the therapist wished to address
was the distortion in the therapeutic alliance. Rather than
patient and therapist thinking together and elaborating
their understanding of the patient's problems, the patient
was telling things without thinking about them, and the
therapist was, in the patient's view, saying things that hurt,
and little collaboration was taking place.

The therapist wished to call the patient's attention to
the problems in the alliance as a prerequisite for beginning
to explore the character pathology. To some extent, these
were inseparable, or put differently, the character pathology was creating problems in the alliance. Without an alli-

ance, however, work on the character issues could not really take place.

> *Therapist:* I have noticed that when I make a comment about what you have been telling me, we don't think or talk much about it together. What have you noticed about your responses to what I say?

This interpretation calls attention to not working together and encourages the patient to observe something about himself. Working together and self-observation are both aspects of the alliance the therapist wants to help the patient develop.

> *Patient:* When you say something, I usually feel you are right on the mark, that you've spotted a problem it hurts to admit to myself. You are very sharp. You know, it's like my wife, she can see right through me.
>
> *Therapist:* You view me as hitting the mark, spotting things, being sharp, hurting you, seeing through you. You must feel like a target rather than someone who will look at yourself with me. Can you imagine us as on the same side?

The therapist uses the patient's self-observations to highlight the way the patient has created a therapeutic relationship in which he is a target rather than a collaborator. The therapist stays with the theme of the alliance, including pointing out the patient's masochistic use of interpretations only insofar as it distorts the working together. Because of the patient's obsessional character and tendency to make every interaction an adversarial one, the therapist's interpretation emphasizes that the patient feels like a target, rather than making himself into a target of the therapist's interpretations. The therapist's comment thus is less of an accusation and, furthermore, emphasizes how the patient feels. In working with obsessional patients, the therapist must help the patient recognize and accept how he feels before showing the patient that he actually creates his "unwanted" feelings, a point developed further in the section on character resistances in Chapter 7. The interpretation ends with an invitation for the patient to think about the therapeutic alliance in everyday terms of being "on the same side," giving the patient a direction for further work on the theme the therapist has isolated.

Summary

This chapter has emphasized the importance of the therapeutic alliance as a way of thinking about how the patient and therapist work together and has presented clinical situations in which problems with the alliance are interpreted. What should be apparent from the examples is the way these interpretations isolate issues of the alliance from other aspects of the therapeutic relationship and from the patient's pathology. For example, the patient who feels hurt by the therapist's interpretations is using the therapy for masochistic gratification and is portraying the therapist as a hurting person, often a sadistically motivated distortion. Furthermore, by demonstrating how much he can "take," he may be expressing certain grandiose ideas about himself, including the idea that he be loved and valued because of his suffering. The meticulous detail in his free associations may be a way of thwarting the therapist's interest in unconscious derivatives, hidden behind the patient's claim of obedience to the therapist's instructions. The details may unconsciously represent feces he piles on top of the therapist, may serve to ridicule the therapist's quest for detail, and may keep forbidden thoughts from entering the patient's mind. The controlling behavior may represent the way the patient felt controlled by a parental figure or the way he controls anyone who threatens him. Many other meanings in the interaction are available for interpretation because all mental events are overdetermined or, put differently, are the outcome of complex compromises among many conflicting mental trends. The interpretations given in the clinical examples in this chapter highlight ways of fostering the alliance and approaching problems that significantly interfere with the conduct of the therapeutic work. It is always a matter of judgment as to what to interpret at any given moment. The discussion emphasizes how to utilize interpretations to foster the development and analyze problems in the therapeutic alliance, a complex but very useful way of conceptualizing the cooperative work the patient and therapist do together. Only when the alliance is functioning adequately can interpretive work on other issues proceed.

——————— Suggested Readings ———————

Brenner, C. (1979). Working alliance, therapeutic alliance, and transference. *Journal of the American Psychoanalytic Association Suppl.* 27:137–158.

> This paper is included because it offers a viewpoint contrary to the usual acceptance of the validity and usefulness of the concept of the therapeutic alliance. Brenner feels, and attempts to show by examination of clinical vignettes purported to illustrate the value of the alliance concept, that alliance issues are really part of the transference and that the alliance concept is, on the whole, neither justifiable nor desirable.

Curtis, H. C. (1979). The concept of therapeutic alliance: Implications for the "Widening Scope." *Journal of the American Psychoanalytic Association Suppl.* 27:159–192.

> The author reviews the historical development of the alliance concept and describes its usefulness in separating the rational and irrational elements in the collaborative aspects of the therapeutic relationship. He discusses the alliance as it pertains to the treatment of more disturbed patients. The paper concludes with an examination of the dangers of focusing exclusively on the alliance as a therapeutic end in itself, which shifts emphasis away from such core concepts as the interpretation of unconscious conflict and transference.

Greenson, R. R. (1965b). The working alliance and the transference neurosis. *Psychoanalytic Quarterly* 34:155–181.

> This paper describes the working alliance as "the relatively non-neurotic, rational rapport which the patient has with his analyst. It is this reasonable and purposeful part of the feelings the patient

has for the analyst that makes for the working alliance" (p. 157). This is contrasted with the regressive, irrational transference manifestations that are, in part, kept separate from the working alliance by the analyst's interpretations. Greenson offers a series of vignettes illustrating the vicissitudes of the alliance in relation to unexpected difficulties in the course of therapy. Contributions to the alliance by the patient, the analyst, and the setting are described. The author emphasizes "humanity" in the analyst as a prerequisite for maintaining the working alliance. Suggestions are offered for restoring the alliance when problems arise.

Sterba, R. F. (1934). The fate of the ego in analytic therapy. *International Journal of Psycho-Analysis* 15:117–126.

This paper describes the split in ego functions that must occur in therapy in order to allow the patient to both experience regression and transference and, simultaneously, reasonably observe himself, a split supported by identifying with the analyst's observing and analyzing functions. This concept serves as the basis for modern ideas about the therapeutic or working alliance.

Zetzel, E. R. (1956). Current concepts of transference. *International Journal of Psycho-Analysis* 37:369–376.

This paper is included here because it is always cited in connection with the author's development of the concept of the therapeutic alliance, although she attributes the idea to Edward Bibring and refers to Sterba's (1934) earlier contribution regarding the division within the ego of the patient that allows the alliance to develop. In fact, the main thrust of Zetzel's paper is to compare and contrast the "classical" and "Kleinian" viewpoints regarding the origins and handling of the transference in analysis.

4

Interpretation of Resistance

The theory of resistance as a technical concept has changed during the development of therapeutic technique. It has evolved from a circumscribed meaning involving a limited array of mental activity toward one encompassing aspects of all mental activity that becomes part of the therapeutic process. To some extent, we no longer speak of resistances per se, but rather attempt to identify the resistance inherent in all the patient's activities. The interpretation of resistance, one of the therapist's main activities, should take into account the potentially resistant aspect of all behavior.

_____ Defining Resistance _____

Resistance as a concept has evolved with the changing views of psychopathological processes. Freud initially viewed repression as a defensive process that keeps traumatic experi-

ences and unacceptable wishes out of conscious awareness.
It was the central psychopathological mechanism. He spoke
of the psychoneuroses of defense. The therapeutic task was
to undo the defense of repression, which would lead to
change and cure. Freud found this a difficult task and he
soon began to recognize those activities of the patient that
interfered with the undoing or lifting of the defensive repression. He recognized that the mental forces that resulted
in defense were mobilized in the treatment process and led
to the difficulties encountered in trying to undo repression.
He labeled these difficulties resistances and saw them as
the therapeutic manifestation of pathological defenses. Thus
defensive operations became resistances as the therapist attacked the former during treatment. To understand the nature of resistance became the way to understand those defensive processes that were at the root of the patient's pathology.

With the development of later psychopathological models
that emphasize unresolved unconscious conflicts and their
distorting influence on the development of the psychic apparatus, all mental processes began to be viewed as serving
multiple functions (Waelder 1930). Thus, one could speak of
the defense function of a particular mental activity, along
with other (i.e., gratifying, delaying, inhibiting, communicating) functions, any of which might at one time be primary.
For example, reflective thinking on the patient's part might
in one instance be cooperative, in another a resistance to free
associating, and in yet another be exhibitionistically gratifying; or it might be all three at once. Resistance becomes that
aspect of all behavior during treatment that stands in opposition to the therapeutic process. It thus even becomes possible to speak of the patient's making progress as a resistance
against deeper exploration of difficulties hidden by the clinical improvement, in practice a very common occurrence.

To summarize, resistance is a way of conceptualizing
those aspects of the patient's activity, conscious and unconscious, which are used to counteract or interfere with
therapeutic progress. It is also useful to include the notion

that resistance is directed against the therapeutic activities of the therapist. The therapist, and the pressure he exerts in the direction of change, or at least in the direction of new and different ways of looking at things, is resisted. In a later discussion of the interpretation of resistance, an expanded conceptualization of resistance will be emphasized. Resistance is one aspect of whatever the patient does in treatment and is directed against the therapist and the pressure he exerts. It is also useful to view resistance as the patient resisting himself. Put another way, the patient is involved in contradictory actions, in a fight with himself, trying to change and trying not to change, trying to clarify and also trying to obscure (Schafer 1973a). Interpretations of resistance formulated in this way take into account its internal conflictual nature.

An underlying theme that grows naturally out of the above considerations concerns the adversarial nature of resistances and often of the therapist's interpretations of resistance. A general principle of interpretation of mental life is respect for the adaptive aspect of all mental events. The very term resistance, conjuring up as it does notions of force and counterforce, highlights the "fight" in resistance. Yet an interpretive stance that "fights" resistance will soon "fight" the patient in a way that rarely leads to the kind of therapeutic climate and dialogue that allows for change in the patient. Keeping in mind the conflictual, the adaptive, the self-defeating, the self-protective, and especially the inevitable, ever present nature of resistance will allow for interpretations that avoid overemphasizing an adversarial position. Resistance must be shown to the patient as something he does, usually unconsciously, to defend or protect himself, to adjust to the threats he perceives, usually in a distorted way, in the direction of the therapeutic work and in the relationship with the therapist. Resistance is of value to the patient, given the way he perceives or experiences himself, the therapist, and the treatment, and thus will only be given up as this is modified by more understanding.

_____ Interpreting Resistance _____

Because resistance is a potential attribute of whatever the patient does in treatment, no wholly satisfying and all-inclusive categorization is possible. Certain types of resistance and their interpretation will be discussed here in order to illustrate those underlying principles of interpretation applicable to the widest variety of treatment situations. In general, an interpretation of resistance should include an understanding of what the resisting activity consists of, what is being resisted, and the reason why the patient needs to resist as he relates to the present treatment configuration as well as what are, to him, its historical antecedents. In practice, this interpretive approach to a resistance occurs in parts and, in many instances, is incomplete. The sequence usually begins with calling the patient's attention to some activity on his part that is interfering with the therapeutic task. In this way, the therapist attempts to make the resistance an object of joint investigation. It becomes an activity of the patient that can, at least temporarily, be seen in isolation from his other activities, that can be consciously acknowledged and talked about, and that can be modified in the interest of therapeutic progress. The resisting behavior can usually be understood as an avoidance of something about which the patient is afraid, ashamed, guilty, or otherwise uncomfortable, although the patient's discomfort may not be conscious. It is usually possible for the therapist to indicate to the patient in a general way the material that is being avoided. The patient's immediate associations following the pointing out of a resistance often indicate what is being warded off. The therapist should attempt to explore the nature of the patient's fears or other reasons for avoidance, accepting the resistance as necessary and understandable in the face of the patient's apprehension. It is the latter that should be questioned and explored first, since this is where many of the patient's distortions and self-deceptions, remnants of both his childhood and adult traumas and poorly resolved conflicts, are most evident. Such exploration usually leads directly into the material's being avoided in a way that maximizes the usefulness of such material. This sequence of interpretive approach, which takes into account the patient's need for resisting and the factors, however unrealistic or distorted, that require it, is most likely to maintain and strengthen the sense of understanding, support, and joint inquiry that will allow the warded off material to enter into the therapeutic dialogue.

The patient, a scientist in his early forties, sought treatment because of the breakup of his marriage and his ensuing depression. His character structure was obsessional and masochistic and soon became the central focus of work in treatment. After an initial period of exploration of current problems and his depressive response to them, the patient began to talk about his angrily submissive relationship with his militaristic father. He examined the ways he re-created this submission in his professional and personal relationships. He described his adult avoidance of openly expressing his assertive, competitive, and ambitious strivings, much as he had with his father, fearing the latter's retaliations should he appear too confrontational or independent. He filled in, with considerable detail, a picture of his father as an insecure, controlling, moralistic parent whose need to dominate his family had alienated all around him. The patient gained more understanding about his resentment of his father and all subsequent authority figures in his life, as well as the indirect ways in which this resentment dominated his current relationships.

For a long time, the therapist felt that the patient's treatment was progressing satisfactorily, but gradually the therapist began to sense a sameness in the material about the patient's father. Little new information was forthcoming, and the patient, who initially was very guilty about saying anything negative about his father, seemed almost too comfortable in relating instance after instance of his father's cruel and unfair domination of his family. The therapist came to believe that what had once been useful exploration of important genetic material had become a resistance against the emergence of new information, particularly about the patient's relationship to his mother. Material about the mother was conspicuously absent from the treatment, despite the patient's early report that his relationship to her was overly close and troublesome to him.

> *Therapist:* I have noticed, and wonder if you have, that as intensely as you remember and talk about your struggles with your father, thoughts and memories about your mother rarely appear for us to look at.
> *Patient:* I don't think I'm hiding anything. She was always around, right in the middle of things, sort of.

There followed a few somewhat forced comments about the patient's mother, which were made in a compliant manner consistent with the patient's need to appease whenever he experienced the therapist as making a demand on him. However, the patient soon reverted to his more stereotyped reiteration of the humiliations and bullying he experienced when interacting with his father and the latter's current surrogates, including the therapist.

> *Therapist:* Despite trying to talk more about your mother, you return to your father as though you can't allow yourself to tell me more about your feelings toward her.
> *Patient:* I feel you want to force me to have an Oedipus complex, whatever that is. The thought of my having sexual feelings toward my mother is disgusting. I was very close, too close to her, maybe, as a child. But it was her doting on me. And it was never sexual. I do remember the way she would wear pajamas around the apartment. But that's all.

There followed a series of increasingly vivid memories indicating the patient's childhood sexual curiosity about his mother. Furthermore, the patient revealed that, even prior to beginning the treatment, he feared the therapist would force him to admit to sexual feelings toward his mother, an admission he vowed to himself he would never make.

> *Therapist:* Part of your fight with yourself about remembering these feelings has centered around your not wanting to be pushed around by me.

Patient: I hate to admit any of this to you, that you are right. I feel like you've caught me doing something naughty, and you will gloat over it.

This clinical example portrays a typical resistance met with in analytic therapies and illustrates certain principles of interpretation. Material that first emerges as an advance in the treatment is lingered over to resist the emergence of new data. (This form of resistance is dynamically similar to that of clinical improvement, which some patients use to justify prematurely terminating treatment to keep more troublesome material out of awareness.) The therapist's first interpretation, or partial interpretation, is to point out to the patient the absence of material about the mother. The therapist makes an observation and encourages the patient to observe himself similarly. There is no accusation, nor any mention of why the material about the mother might be missing. The emphasis is on observing together, rather than on criticizing the patient. Nonetheless, the patient's first response is to claim innocence, which offers a clue about one motive for hiding or withholding material, namely, guilt. In keeping with the patient's superficially compliant attitude toward the therapist, the patient attempts to focus on mother, but soon reverts to father. The therapist's second intervention takes into account the patient's conscious cooperative efforts, but points out that the patient, despite his efforts, returns to the by now more comfortable material. This interpretation portrays the patient's resistance as a struggle with himself that involves an internal prohibition. The patient responds by attempting to place one side of his conflict about feelings toward his mother into the therapist. It is not that the patient has sexual feelings about his mother. Rather, the therapist is forcing the patient to say things that are untrue, presumably because of the therapist's imagined need to force the patient into some model the therapist has about the basis of psychopathology. Next, the patient reveals his disgust at the thought of the sexual nature of his feelings toward his mother. In fact, the therapist had made no mention

of sexual material. The patient goes on to develop the material held back, his "too close" relationship to his mother, her
provocativeness, his sexual curiosity. The therapist, after a
time, returns to the resistance, the patient feeling forced,
"pushed around," the latter the patient's term for what au-
thorities always do to him. Here, one motive for resisting
emerges as clearly integral to the material that has been held
back or avoided. The patient experiences the therapist's
searching or exploratory attitude as competitive, with a
winner who will gloat at being correct, and also as spying on
the patient's private "naughty" activities, all motives, feelings, fantasies, and worries connected with the Oedipal material being defended against. This is a good example of how
the act of resisting and its motives are intimately bound up
with the material being warded off. The resistance should
never be circumvented, because in doing so much valuable
material will be bypassed. If the resistance is explored without criticism, and within an intrapsychic conflictual context, the patient will eventually come to value the exploration of his resistances as a valuable source of information
about himself. The connections among the various conflicting motives inherent in the resistance and in the material
being resisted should be stressed in subsequent interpretations. This helps the patient experience the interconnected-
ness of all mental events, the realization of which always
helps the patient to feel less frightened and guilty about his
resisting behavior.

   In summary, in this clinical vignette, the therapist first
points out the conspicuous absence of certain material and
encourages the patient to observe that he is resisting. When
this becomes clear, the therapist begins to portray the resistance as the patient in conflict with himself. This non-
accusatory approach allows the warded off material to
emerge, along with information about the motives for its
being defended against. The therapist attends to both the
resistance and the new material and will subsequently tie
the two together when possible. It should be noted that the
therapist needed to repeat the initial part of the interpreta-

tion. It is often necessary to repeat, or restate in a slightly different way, an interpretation. Beginning therapists often "try" an interpretation once and then back off because they are insecure about whether they are correct or because they fear they are badgering the patient or being too aggressive. Interpretations of resistance should be a consistent activity of the therapist throughout the treatment. Many examples of interpretation of resistance will be presented in other chapters. In the following section, the interpretation of silence, a common early resistance in treatment, will be discussed to illustrate further those general principles of interpretation applicable to all resistances that may arise in the treatment situation.

_____ Interpreting Silence, a Special Resistance _____

During any treatment, there are periods when the patient will be silent. Despite the "rule" that the patient say whatever comes to mind, we know that there will be times when the patient will be thinking about something, recalling an event, mulling over his responses to an interpretation, or perhaps experiencing some intense emotion. We know that such silences are necessary and desirable in order that the patient be allowed to experience, reflect, recall, formulate, in effect, to participate both cognitively and emotionally in the therapeutic dialogue. In fact, certain patients defensively talk non-stop, under the guise of free associating, to avoid feeling, thinking about, or responding to interpretations. The request or rule that the patient "think out loud" is only meant to approximate as free and uncensored an attitude as possible toward reporting thoughts and feelings during sessions. Silences have many meanings and purposes. They should not be thought of exclusively as resistances. Nonetheless, most prolonged periods of silence include important elements of resistance and should be interpreted in a manner consistent with the principles of interpretation of resistance.

Silences are particularly difficult for beginning therapists
to deal with for a number of reasons. Most resistances gradually increase the tension between the patient and therapist
until they are resolved. With silence, this tension is immediate and inescapable. It is not possible for the therapist to
listen to further material before deciding what to do. Silence
calls for action, some kind of intervention. If the case is
being presented to a supervisor, the silence robs the therapist of material to present. Furthermore, the therapist cannot wait to ask the supervisor what to do. Therapists struggle during their training to learn to listen, to wait, to let the
patient take the lead, to understand, to be objective, to link
past and present. When a therapist is listening carefully and
patiently while trying to understand the material, he feels
relatively secure even if he is unsure of what the material
means or what to interpret. If the patient is silent, the therapist cannot do any of the above. The pressure to act often
leads to a number of unhelpful or counterproductive interventions. One group of such interventions might be described
as efforts to get the patient talking again. These include
interventions like "What is on your mind?" "What are you
thinking about?" "You were describing your reaction to. . . ."
"Perhaps you can tell me some more about. . . ." Implicit in
them is the recognition that the silence is distressing and
that it should be ended. Yet such comments are intended to
bypass a resistance rather than to explore it and thus violate
a general principle of interpretation. Another counterproductive response frequently observed among inexperienced
and sometimes even experienced therapists is to sit silently
with the patient for prolonged periods of time. Because learning to be quiet is highly valued as an integral part of becoming a therapist, remaining quiet during the patient's
silence can feel like an accomplishment, a mastering of a
tense period of time without having to act to relieve one's
own discomfort. Such an attitude leads to "waiting it out"
with patients and results in much wasted time. Patients
often experience such silent "interchanges" as struggles or
contests, abandonments, or periods of joint helplessness.

When such feelings are reinforced by repeated periods of lengthy silent "standoffs," exploration of the silence, if and when it finally does occur, centers on these feelings. Although they may themselves be revealing and valuable to explore with the patient, they are, to some extent, iatrogenically or artificially induced, and may obscure the original basis or meaning of the silence.

Silences usually seem longer than they actually are, and there is no rule of thumb to decide how long a silence should be allowed to continue. In fact, even if the patient spontaneously resumes speaking, most lengthy silences are worth exploring and interpreting. In general, a minute or two is probably as long as any silence should be allowed to continue without efforts made to explore its meaning.

The first step in interpreting a silence, especially early in treatment, is to make the silence the object of a mutual, noncritical exploration. The patient is not to be blamed for being silent, nor is the resumption of free association to be defined as the immediate or most important goal in intervening. The silence, as with any resistance, must become a source of useful information about the patient's inner life. In time it is hoped that the patient will begin to observe when he becomes silent and will explore, on his own initiative, what has interrupted his free associations. In fact, it is often the case that the patient's first psychodynamically informed self-observing and self-analyzing experiences in treatment occur in wondering about the meaning of silent periods, provided early silences have been correctly handled by the therapist.

> The patient, a married grade-school teacher in her late thirties, came for treatment because of a chronic depression that had recently been so severe as to interfere seriously with her ability to do her job and with her relationships with peers and students at work. During early sessions, she described current difficulties in her work, her friendships, and her marriage. She spoke of herself in a very disparaging, critical, and unforgiving way and described the low regard in which she believed she was held by her colleagues.

Once she had outlined in a general way her current problems, she had increasing difficulty speaking freely during the sessions. She began each session by filling the therapist in on recent developments in her life and then became silent. She was distressed and uncomfortable during these silences, and then apologetic and self-critical about them.

Patient: I'm sorry. I feel like I don't have anything to say. (Silence, lasting a minute or two.)
Therapist: Let's try to understand the silence together and see what it tells us about you.
Patient: I just seem to run out of things to say. (Silence.)
Therapist: When you run out of things to say, how do you begin to feel?
Patient: I feel stupid. In fact, often, in the car on the way over here, I worry about whether I'll have enough things to talk about to fill the time.
Therapist: You feel stupid.
Patient: After I've told you the news since my last appointment, I can't think of anything important to tell you. My mind wanders to dumb things, what to cook for dinner, my hair, stupid things like that.
Therapist: You label your more personal thoughts dumb or stupid. What does that bring to mind?
Patient: My parents. They were always telling me I was stupid, that my opinions were stupid if they were different from theirs.
Therapist: So when you are silent, you keep more personal things to yourself. I think you may do this to ward off the possibility that I, too, may find your more personal thoughts stupid, even if that doesn't consciously occur to you.
Patient: You know, I do worry that you'll think I'm stupid, although I never put that together with being silent. Stupid was a word my mother used constantly. She still does, whenever I don't do things her way.

In this example, the therapist begins by describing the silence as something valuable, a source of information rather than as a problem, something to be understood together. The therapist, aware of the patient's intensely self-critical nature, draws the patient's attention to her feelings when the silences occur. Her report that she feels stupid leads easily to the interpretation that she may unconsciously attribute an equally critical attitude to the therapist. This leads naturally to the patient's associations about her parents' criticisms of her, now internalized as part of her character structure and readily attributed to people with whom she currently interacts. Much subsequent work needed to be done on this issue, work begun through interpretation of silence as a resistance. The patient explored subsequent silences along similar lines, amplifying on her constant fear of being seen as stupid with a deepening understanding of her own, unduly harsh, self-critical tendencies.

> The patient, an unmarried graduate student in his late twenties, came for treatment because of loneliness and serious problems in getting along with people. He felt relatively friendless and was depressed and angry most of the time. The patient found it difficult to free associate almost from the outset. Other than giving a historical account of his life, he was often unable to speak during the sessions. He attempted to draw the therapist into asking questions, which he would then answer in a dry, matter-of-fact way or in a manner that indicated his feeling that the question was foolish, off the mark, or too obvious and superficial. The tension during the sessions, which were dominated by long, frustrating silences, was very wearing on both participants. The therapist was, in fact, puzzled that the patient came so willingly to sessions and genuinely seemed to want to derive some gain from the therapy, yet was unable or unwilling to speak very much about himself.
>
> The patient, in describing his past, told of losing his mother during his infancy. He was raised by his father and a series of housekeepers. He reported a very unsatisfactory relationship with his father, with whom he felt he could not talk. On one occasion, he described a typical phone conversation with his father. When asked how things were going, the patient told his father that he was lonely, depressed, and thinking of dropping out of graduate school. His father commented that "things can get rough like that sometimes"

and then proceeded to tell the patient a series of trivial details about relatives who were moving, about his new office furniture, and about the family dog, ending the conversation without any further mention of the patient's distress. The patient said that he had become used to such interactions with his father, that they still made him angry, but that he had given up trying to change them.

Efforts to help the patient examine his difficulty in speaking freely led the patient to defensively claim he was a "concrete" sort of person, that he had no thoughts while silent, no fantasies or daydreams, but was totally blank.

> *Patient:* I'm not thinking anything. Unless I have a concrete subject, nothing comes to mind. This is hopeless.
> *Therapist:* Hopeless?
> *Patient:* Hopeless. (Silence.)
> *Therapist:* Hopeless is the word you used to describe talking to your father.
> *Patient:* (Silence.)

The therapist, having unsuccessfully tried "to get the patient talking" and having used "waiting it out" strategies in the past, found himself thinking further about the patient's hopeless phone conversations with his father. He thought that the patient was recreating with his silence some aspect of this hopeless interaction.

> *Therapist:* I suspect that you are silent with me in order not to tell me something important about yourself, only to have me react the way your father might, and that you hide this even from yourself by believing you are concrete and have nothing on your mind.
> *Patient:* You haven't been of much help to me so far. (Silence.) This is sort of like talking to him. You know, I thought last time that your way of saying "time's up" was like the way he ends our phone calls, "got to go now," after I've listened to all the garbage about nothing that he tells me.

> *Therapist:* I take it you have given up telling him anything that matters much to you.
> *Patient:* It's like he wants to believe everything is fine anyway.

The patient continued talking about his inability to communicate with his father. The more he talked about this, the angrier he became. Further work on the silence revealed that the patient was indeed avoiding the possibility that the therapist might respond to his distress the way his father responded. Should this happen, he felt certain he would become so angry he would leave a treatment he felt was his only chance of changing himself.

In this clinical example, the patient, because of the serious nature of his difficulties, very quickly recreated in the treatment his non-communicative "hopeless" relationship with his father. The therapist interpreted the silence, which because of its global nature interfered with any progress in the treatment, in terms of information available about the father. The intensity of the difficulty required a transference interpretation very early in the treatment, without much certainty on the therapist's part. Such situations are not uncommon in the treatment of seriously disturbed patients. With such patients, the transference develops very rapidly and is difficult for the patient to recognize as a distortion. In this case, the silence was a transference resistance, in that it recreated aspects of a past relationship and seriously interfered with the treatment. The patient responded by revealing how very angry his father's unwillingness to really hear his distress made him, and subsequently confirmed the therapist's interpretation about the silence being a way of avoiding a similar event in the treatment.

It should be mentioned, in terms of general principles of interpretation, that, in this instance, the therapist was far from certain about the content or correctness of his intervention. With seriously disturbed patients and patients in crises, for whom prolonged silence in treatment is a subtype, interpretations must be made without the certainty that comes from an in-depth knowledge of the patient and the particular issue at hand. The time-worn dictum that it is best to wait until one is relatively certain about an interpretation is not always applicable and is itself a dictum open to modification or at least amendment. With very disturbed patients in crises, and even in some healthier obsessional patients who would like to be certain of everything, a speculative or tentative interpretation is far preferable to inactivity, which may confirm the patient's worst fears about there being no hope, no way of explaining or understanding. In crises, a plausible explanation, even if later modified or even rejected, helps to organize and objectify the situation. Even in less critical situations, patients appreciate the therapist's attempts to understand and explain, as long as the interpretations are thoughtful and based on the available information. They may lead the patient to change, add to, or refute what the therapist has said, in order to arrive at a more accurate interpretation. This is preferable to a therapist who is or feels the need to "always be right."

Many other reasons for silences can be understood in terms of resistance. Especially common is the silence as a way of not expressing negative feelings toward the therapist or of waiting until sexual or other embarrassing or uncomfortable material "passes from one's mind." The therapist should treat each silence as an activity on the patient's part that represents a compromise among conflicting trends.

> The patient, a young woman with many phobias and anxiety symptoms, was in the second year of her treatment when the following occurred: The therapist was uncharacteristically late for a session. The patient was unable to say anything. She sat silently with her usual pleasant expression, but began cracking her knuckles, a signal familiar to both the patient and therapist, based on past work together, that the patient was angry. Despite the patient obviously noting what she had been doing and smiling self-consciously, she remained silent.

> *Therapist:* My lateness and your silence must be related.
> *Patient:* I guess I am angry about it. (Silence.)

Therapist: Your being silent must feel somehow safer to you than telling me about being angry at me.

Patient: I don't feel it's safe to get angry at you, although I know that's ridiculous. I wanted you to know I was angry. In fact, I wanted to make you guilty by seeing how you had upset me so much that I couldn't talk.

Therapist: By being silent, you could punish me without having to risk being openly angry.

Patient: I didn't feel I had a right to be angry. You're never late, so I'm sure you couldn't help it. Maybe what I was afraid of was your telling me something terrible happened which made you late. Then I'd feel awful. Same old me. You know how little it takes to make me feel guilty.

In this example, the therapist calls the patient's attention to the connection between the silence and the therapist's lateness. Even though the connection is obvious, putting it into words is useful in helping the patient acquire some distance from the silence. Getting the patient to express her obvious anger, as, for example, by saying "you must be angry at me for being late," would bypass the reason for being silent about it. Thus, the therapist, instead, calls attention to the patient's need for the silence, that expressing anger somehow makes the patient feel unsafe. This leads to the explanation of the silence as a compromise formation in which the patient's anger takes the form of punishing the therapist indirectly in order to avoid being made to feel guilty, a compromise easily tied to other activities on the patient's part inside and outside the treatment.

Many other types of silence occur during treatment. Silence may be a way of remembering some event that occurred silently, or as in one patient, a way of recreating her relationship with a beloved silent grandparent, aphasic for many years following a stroke. Silence may be teasing or retaliatory, withholding or reflective. Usually a strong element of resistance is part of the basis for silence. Interpretations of this resistant element should take into account the patient's need for the silence and the compromise it represents among various mental trends. The silence should become an object of mutual observation and should be viewed as a valuable source of information, not merely as something to be tolerated, waited out, or ended to "get on with things."

Summary

Resistance has been described as a complex phenomenon or group of phenomena arising within the treatment situation. There are several ways to conceptualize resistance profitably. Each has its place in determining the interpretive interventions that are designed to overcome resistance as an obstacle to therapeutic progress, perhaps its most general conceptualization. Resistances are the clinical counterpart of intrapsychic defensive operations and appear when these defensive operations are threatened by the work of treatment. Thus, to understand a resistance is to gain valuable information about the patient's defensive operations. This leads naturally to the idea that interpretations should portray resistances as valuable sources of information about intrapsychic events rather than merely as obstacles to be overcome.

Resistances are in some way directed at the therapist's activities against which the patient, due to important distortions, feels he must protect himself. Interpretations must reflect an appreciation of the patient's feeling that he needs to defend himself as well as explore those distortions that underlie the patient's fearfulness. It is usually in the nature of such fearful distortions that information about what is being warded off can be obtained. Such connections between the nature of warding off and what is being warded off should be linked in subsequent interpretations.

Resistance demonstrates the patient in conflict with himself. Patients both want to reveal and to hide, to change and to remain the same. On one side are the fears, distortions, and traumas of childhood, on the other the patient's hopeful, mature, reality-oriented strengths. The latter are always present or there is no treatment. Presenting interpretations about resistance in terms of the patient in conflict with himself helps to strengthen the therapeutic alliance by calling attention to the patient's rational, therapeutic efforts he is himself undermining, efforts that are easily lost sight of as the tension around resistances and ensuing therapeutic stalemates increases.

Resistance is really only one of many aspects of any activity that is called "the resistance." All mental events have multiple functions. Thus, a silence can be a stubborn withholding, a gratifying victory, a reenactment of a past event, a self-defeating activity, a communication of danger, and many other things, all at once. The time-worn dictum to interpret resistance before content really is misleading. Resistance has content, many contents. What is important is not to avoid, bypass, or devalue resistances. To do so misses their varied and important content, in addition to failing to take into account the patient's fearful need to resist in the first place.

Suggested Readings

Arlow, J. A. (1961). Silence and the theory of technique. *Journal of the American Psychoanalytic Association* 9:44–55.

> Silences occurring within the therapeutic process are dichotomized as silences that serve primarily the function of defense and silences that serve primarily the function of discharge. Arlow describes, in a clear and organized fashion, the many different dynamic meanings of silence, especially evocative and communicative functions within the transference relationship. The therapist's interpretations of silences are portrayed as altering the relationship of forces between discharge and defensive aspects of the silence. Suggestions are offered about optimal directions of interpretation depending on the primary intrapsychic and transference meaning or purpose of the silence.

Greenson, R. R. (1961). On the silence and sounds of the analytic hour. *Journal of the American Psychoanalytic Association* 9:79–84.

> This paper presents several vignettes of analytic hours in which different meanings of silence can be discerned. The author em-

phasizes prolonged silence following interpretations as indicating that the interpretations were incorrect or poorly timed. He also notes the varying responses patients have to the therapist's way of dealing with silences. Greenson notes that the patient cannot help but communicate some of the underlying meanings of the silence in body language. He stresses the communicative as well as the defense functions of silence, both requiring interpretation.

Schafer, R. (1968). The mechanisms of defence. *International Journal of Psycho-Analysis* 49:49–62.

Schafer characterizes defenses as dynamic compromises among conflicting mental trends that allow for gratification as well as inhibition of partially warded off wishes and fantasies. As such, interpretations of defenses must take into account all elements of the compromise in order to be complete and effective. Examples are provided to illustrate the author's thesis.

Schafer, R. (1973a). The idea of resistance. *International Journal of Psycho-Analysis* 54:259–285.

This paper describes resistance in terms of the patient's psychic activity, in keeping with the author's reformulation of psychoanalytic propositions in the language of actions rather than in the mechanistic terms of traditional Freudian metapsychology. Schafer develops a view of resistance as the patient deceiving himself; the patient in conflict with himself as well as with the therapist and the therapeutic work. Such a view of resistance leads to many useful ways of formulating interpretations. Schafer also examines the negative or adversarial view of resistance, explores its historical roots, and makes many useful suggestions about interpreting resistance in a manner that takes into account its affirmative, positive purposes, or put differently, its multiple dynamic functions.

Stone, L. (1973). On resistance to the psychoanalytic process. *Psychoanalysis and Contemporary Science* 2:42–73.

This paper provides a useful overview of the traditional or classical psychoanalytic concept of resistance and its relationship to defense. (Stone's work repays careful study but presupposes considerable familiarity with the psychoanalytic literature and with psychoanalytic "jargon.") The author delineates two broad groups of resistances, "tactical" resistances, the ego's manifest resisting actions, and "strategic" resistances, those silent impediments to the progress or successful termination of treatment that are based on more central and deep-seated vulnerabilities in the psychic apparatus and that threaten disorganization of the psychic structure in the face of the therapeutic work. Stone describes the relationship of resistance to transference, contrasting transference resistances and resistance to the emergence of transference.

Waelder, R. (1930). The principle of multiple function. *Psychoanalytic Quarterly* 5:45–62, 1936.

This classic psychoanalytic paper summarizes the thesis that all mental events serve multiple functions as psychic compromises. This principle is useful in the interpretive process in formulating interpretations that take into account the more hidden aspects of certain mental phenomena in addition to their more obvious or conscious intent or purpose.

5

Interpretation of Transference

Transference was recognized as an aspect of psychotherapeutic work by Freud as early as 1895 (Breuer and Freud 1895). Initially, he viewed transference as an obstacle met with in treatment, an obstacle he characterized as a false connection or mental mistake in which the therapist is substituted for some important past figure as the object of a patient's repressed wish or feeling. Even in his first discussion of transference as an obstacle to be overcome, Freud noted that the distressing affects associated with the repressed material could be worked out equally well in relation to the original object or to a substitute object, the therapist, in the transference. This is a useful way of conceptualizing the role of the transference in the treatment process and has served as a basis for the evolution of ideas about the nature and value of transference in all analytic psychotherapies. Transference is now seen as central to the therapeutic action of analytic treatment. In terms of technique, transference interpretations are among the most important interventions the therapist makes. Yet transference is by no means an easy concept to understand, and similarly, transference interpretations are at times difficult to make. These difficulties often reflect uncertainty or lack of clarity about what transference really is, how it takes shape in the treatment process, and what its relationship is to more general interpersonal distortions.

Psychoanalytic theories of psychopathology are rooted in the idea that the past distorts the present, that past difficulties are continually repeated, and that recovery is based upon uncovering old conflicts and resolving them in such a way that their distorting influence is abolished. The patient can be expected to distort his important adult relationships significantly, in a way that conforms to the structure of his unconscious difficulties, which usually have to do with his conflict-ridden relationships to his parents during the formative years of development. Thus, a patient, raised by intensely rigid and controlling parents who could not tolerate any rebelliousness or independent thinking in their child, might be likely to experience, as an adult, a spouse's or an employer's reasonable request as an arbitrary and controlling demand, stirring up all the anger and resentment of his childhood. Such distortions need not be limited to people with significant psychopathology. All personal interactions are colored by past experiences that shape current expectations and responses. Especially conflictual and unsatisfying relationships with parents and other influential figures from the childhood years have a particularly lasting and distorting influence on people's adult relationships. How can one relate such ubiquitous distortions to the concept of transference in a manner that ensures that the latter term will keep its specific clinical meaning? Transference is the manifestation, within the psychotherapeutic relationship, of the ubiquitous distorting influence of past relationships on current ones, intensified by the regressive forces inherent in the treatment situation and clarified by the therapist's neutrality, relative anonymity, and objectivity in the face of the patient's distorted view of him. The therapist, by virtue of his objectivity, experience, and expertise, is able to interpret these transference distortions in a manner that maximizes their usefulness. They become a means of understanding and influencing the way the patient's past, recreated in the transference, interferes with the patient's current life. The transference is thus a means of knowing the past by re-experiencing it in relation to the therapist, as well as a vehicle for change insofar as distortions of the past are corrected by interpretations that bring adult insights to childhood conflictual relationships. Although the mental tendency to repeat the past by distorting the present occurs throughout life in all significant relationships, transference refers to the special instance of this repetition with the therapist. Transference interpretations use this repetition in the patient's behalf.

Early Transference Interpretations

In discussing transference interpretations, three phases of interpretive work will be described for the sake of clarity, and to separate technical issues. In actual clinical work, these phases overlap considerably, and no attempt should be made to adhere rigidly to the sequence described. The first phase, early transference interpretations, concerns the handling of those early signs of the idiosyncratic distortions the therapist can detect in the patient's response to him. Immediate technical issues are raised in how to respond to these early manifestations of transference. One concerns the widely held, often repeated dictum that the transference should only be interpreted when it begins to interfere with the progress of the treatment, when it becomes a resistance. A related notion is that focusing too soon on transference interferes with its further development. There are those who disagree with these traditional ideas about early transference interpretations (see especially Gill and Muslin 1976), but for the most part, these views have resulted in a cautious approach to early transference phenomena. Although such caution is, in fact, wise, these "rules" are deceiving and should not be considered proven principles of interpretation. Mostly they are based upon responses to less than optimal transference interpretations that make the patient anxious, guilty, confused, self-conscious, or otherwise defensive. If early transference interpretations are correctly handled, they deepen the therapeutic alliance, lead to an increasingly safe environment for the development of more intense transference manifestations, and lay the groundwork for later, more complete, and far-reaching transference interpretations.

One important interpretive issue often handled incorrectly concerns the very nature of transference and stems from Freud's earliest views on the subject (Breuer and Freud 1895), a view he corrected in his later writings (see especially Freud 1912a). Therapists often interpret transference as though the feelings or attitudes that provide the basis for such interpretations are, in fact, mistakes and are really directed toward someone else. Thus, one hears interpretations such as "you're not really angry at me, you're angry at your father," or "you see me as disinterested or bored when in fact you feel your parents didn't care about you." Such interpretations, which unfortunately are quite common, especially among inexperienced therapists, seem to tell patients that what they are feeling is not real, that they are mistaken. Such interpretations may be taken by the patient as admonishments not to continue to direct feelings toward the therapist that apply to others. Freud eventually recognized that when the patient, in the transference, falls in love with the therapist, it is the therapist, and no one else, the patient loves. Interpretations that tell patients that their feelings are not real get nowhere. Patients to whom such interpretations are made rightly feel misunderstood and pushed away and often become very reluctant to make subsequent transference feelings known. Correctly made early transference interpretations call to the patient's attention certain aspects of their emotional attitudes as reflecting the patient's current feelings, perhaps highlighting some particular intensity, contradiction, or anxiety about such feelings, and inviting further inquiry. Interpretations made in this way do not interfere with transference development and allow the transference work to take place without always requiring that the resistant element of the transference be predominant.

> Early in the analytic treatment of a very rigid, obsessional graduate student, the therapist became increasingly aware of the patient's tendency to wince and swallow hard each time the therapist began an interpretation. The patient spoke at great length about his distant and difficult relationship with his father. Most of his memories of interactions with his father centered around those rare times when his father sought him out to speak to him, almost always involving some criticism, warning, or punishment. The patient reported his remembered dread whenever his father wished to speak with him and would often grimace when describing his father's perceived unyielding demandingness and cruelty. The therapist connected this in his thinking with the patient's anticipatory wincing in response to his interpretations and with many other indications of the development of a paternal transference. The patient regularly seemed surprised by the therapist's fairness and consideration for his feelings. The patient was very careful in what he said, as though perpetually expecting criticism. The therapist decided to call the patient's attention to the developing paternal transference by making him aware of his involuntary grimacing as the therapist began to speak.

> *Therapist:* Each time I begin to say something to you, you wince as though you expect me to say something to hurt you just the way you always expected your father would.
> *Patient:* I didn't know I did that. I do notice I feel anxious when you start to say something.

The patient's subsequent associations centered on his fear of his father and of the therapist. This kind of early transference interpretation is useful in that it accustoms the patient to drawing parallels between the therapeutic relationship and important relationships from the past. Such

interpretations encourage the patient to feel comfortable in
exploring feelings toward the therapist by virtue of the
therapist's interest in and talking directly about such feelings. The therapist's non-critical interpretation helped the
patient to amplify on his fear of the therapist and of his
father. A brief time later, the patient commented that the
therapist had misunderstood something the patient had told
him. The therapist observed that the patient became somewhat defensive after this, accusing himself of perhaps having
been vague to explain the therapist's not having correctly
understood what he was saying. The patient had spoken
often of his father's not being able to tolerate being criticized. The therapist was aware that the patient took great
care to avoid being critical, although, despite his considerable efforts, a critical undertone could be detected behind
much of what he said about others.

> *Therapist:* You appear to have felt you were criticizing me
> and quickly took the blame yourself as though you felt that
> I would automatically get angry with you if you said some-
> thing negative about me, just as your father would.

Interpretations around early negative transference manifestations are extremely important. Although not directly
inviting negative feelings, such interpretations indirectly
make these feelings the subject of mutual interest and investigation. More direct invitations, as in comments like "it
is all right to be angry at me" often backfire because they
attempt to bypass rather than explore the patient's difficulties with such negative feelings. The sample interpretations
presented so far neither discount the patient's feelings by
viewing them as "really directed toward someone else" nor
artificially encourage their expression via statements of permission. They accept the inevitability of transference feelings and explore them within the context of what is known
about the patient's past interpersonal problems. The therapist's openness in talking about transference manifestations
in this way allows for the deepening or intensification of

such feelings and encourages the patient's interest in examining what they reveal about the continuity between past and present.

To summarize, early transference interpretations, if made correctly, identify developing distortions in the patient's emotional view of the therapist. They highlight particularly intense, contradictory, surprising, or uncomfortable aspects of the patient's responses to the therapist. They draw parallels, when possible, between these therapeutic phenomena and similar occurrences in the patient's outside life, both past and present. Such interpretations need not take place only during periods of resistance, but should also be part of the regular therapeutic work. In this way, the patient becomes accustomed to using the therapeutic relationship as a vehicle for recreating and reexperiencing his past. If these early transference interpretations are neither critical, in the sense of indicating that the patient should not see the therapist in a distorted way, nor discounting of the reality of the patient's feelings, in the sense of labeling such responses as "really" directed toward someone else, then such interpretations result in the deepening and elaboration, rather than the inhibition, of the transference development.

Care should be taken that early transference interpretations do not go too deep, in the sense of advancing too far beyond the patient's memory and understanding of his childhood experiences. At times, only parallels with current relationships outside the treatment can be drawn, with connections to the past being left for a later time. Early transference interpretations should stay with the predominant themes in the material, even if less obvious and at least temporarily more peripheral transference manifestations are observed by the therapist. The therapist should pay careful attention to the patient's responses to early transference interpretations to be certain that they encourage an openness and freedom in the patient's expression of feelings about the therapist. Signs of constriction or defensiveness about such feelings after early transference interpretations should be explored, rather than viewed as indicating that the inter-

pretations were incorrect, poorly timed, or otherwise unhelpful. Early negative transference manifestations should
be interpreted in a way that legitimizes and values such
phenomena as sources of useful information. A tendency to
gloss over such negative material, supposedly to maximize
or encourage the development of a positive therapeutic alliance, in fact, obscures important material and intensifies the
patient's later resistance when such negative material, by
virtue of its greater intensity, is interpreted. It should be
noted that with some patients, particularly those with borderline and narcissistic character pathology, powerfully intense transference reactions occur very early in therapy and
require interpretive interventions usually reserved for later
stages in the treatment of more typically neurotic patients.
Aspects of such interventions will be discussed in Chapter 7.

Middle Phase Transference Interpretations

As analytic therapy proceeds with most patients, transference manifestations become more pronounced and transference interpretations become a more central aspect of the
therapeutic work. It is important to comment at this point on
some distinctions frequently made among therapies broadly
grouped as analytically oriented, for purposes of presenting
general principles of transference interpretation. The more
often the sessions are scheduled, and the longer the treatment is expected to last, the more intense transference reactions tend to be and the more useful they become in the
therapeutic uncovering and resolution of unresolved unconscious conflict. In psychoanalysis proper, when sessions
occur four or five times a week for several years, transference phenomena occupy the central position in the work of
treatment. Many analysts have argued that true transference
occurs only in analysis. They believe that what occurs in
psychotherapy should be labeled transient transference
phenomena or that some other term should be used to
separate more superficial transference responses from the

deeper transference presumed to occur only in analysis. Similarly, the concept of transference neurosis indicating a more or less structured "illness" in the therapeutic relationship to replace the patient's neurotic difficulties in his outside life is thought of, in some analytic circles, as unique to psychoanalysis proper. Resolution of this transference neurosis in analysis becomes the mode of therapeutic action of the treatment. In fact, from a clinical standpoint, such distinctions do not hold true. One sometimes sees intense and relatively stable transference phenomena in even brief psychotherapies, as well as cases in analysis in which a transference neurosis as such is difficult to isolate or recognize. In general, analysis allows for the fullest development and use of transference phenomena as a basis for interpretation. In briefer, less intensive psychotherapies, transference phenomena tend to be more fragmentary and often more difficult to explore with the same thoroughness. However, the clinical material, rather than any arbitrary distinctions, should govern the nature, frequency, timing, and depth of interpretations of transference in any therapy. In the discussion that follows, no distinction will be made between different types of analytic treatments. It should be understood that all the phenomena discussed may not occur in every treatment.

TRANSFERENCE RESISTANCE

If during the beginning phase of the treatment, early transference interpretations such as those described in the previous section were judiciously presented, the patient should become accustomed to monitoring the therapeutic relationship for indications of disturbing or surprising emotional reactions that might provide useful information about himself. Yet inevitably, the therapist will notice the gradual development of more constant, unyielding aspects of the patient's distortions of the therapeutic relationship, distortions that interfere with the progress of the work and threaten to undermine the therapeutic alliance. They may be obvious or subtle. The transference may be said to have become a resistance. The interpretation of transference resistance usually plays a large part in the work of the middle phase of all analytic treatments. There is always a resistant element in transference, in that transference implies a re-experiencing of an emotional tie rather than objectively exploring such a tie with the therapist. However, the resistant aspect may at times be secondary. Transference feelings may also affect the patient's early cooperativeness with the therapist or they may allow the patient to feel safely distant from the therapist in order to ward off unrealistic fears about intimacy that might otherwise threaten to destroy the treatment. The term transference resistance should be used in connection with therapeutic developments in which the transference becomes a major and lasting impediment to the progress of treatment, an occurrence that typically takes place only after the treatment has been going on for some time. The following clinical vignette illustrates a typical instance of transference resistance during the middle phase of treatment.

> The patient, a 45-year-old mother of three, came for analytic treatment because of marital difficulties and longstanding problems in her relationship with her parents. She functioned well in her job and was quite successful, although she described deriving little pleasure from her work. She was proud of her children and almost discounted her own achievements. She superficially blamed herself for her marital problems and, in general, had few areas of positive regard for herself other than her ability to persevere in the face of adversity and to work hard.
>
> Early in the treatment of this patient, the therapist observed that the patient would occasionally react to interpretations in a sullen and hurt manner, which seemed similar to her description of her responses to her mother's criticisms. These instances were interpreted to the patient and usually led to further elaboration of both her hostile, guilty, overly dependent relationship with her masochistic mother and her powerful identification with her mother.

As the treatment progressed and the therapeutic regression deepened, the patient became more and more entrenched in sadomasochistic struggles with the therapist, without much evidence of what had initially seemed to be her cooperative interest in the treatment. The patient complained that coming to sessions, given all she had to do on her job and with her children, had become an unfair burden due to scheduling based only on the therapist's convenience. It seemed to the therapist that the patient viewed all his interpretations as evidence that he misunderstood her and therefore continually hurt her feelings. The therapist recognized that the patient was repeating, in her relationship to him, her angry submission to what she felt were her mother's unreasonable, self-centered demands and criticisms. The transference had become a powerful resistance in that interpretations were experienced by the patient as such sadistic attacks that their content was entirely avoided.

The interpretive work on this transference resistance was initially directed toward calling the patient's attention to the way in which the entire interaction with the therapist had become characterized by feelings of being hurt, neglected, misunderstood, or otherwise mistreated. The therapist drew a parallel between the therapeutic relationship and the antecedent childhood relationship between the patient and her mother.

Therapist: How often we see that you respond to my comments by feeling painfully forced to agree that I am correct, much as you told me about having to agree with your mother's peculiar views about things as a child in order to ward off her temper tantrums.

Interpretations such as this one were extensions of interpretations made earlier in the treatment when the patient's transference responses were more fleeting. Similar interpretations were repeated in order to help the patient observe the transference distortions, not an easy task for a patient in the middle of a serious transference resistance. The therapist simultaneously encouraged the patient to bring out as much material as she could remember about similar childhood experiences with her mother, in order to facilitate her being able to see the present as a new version of an old pattern of interaction.

Despite the patient's becoming increasingly familiar with the parallel between her submission to her mother and her felt submission to her therapist, there was as yet little change in the character of the therapeutic relationship other than the patient's being able to use interpretations to facilitate thinking about herself. One might say that the therapeutic alliance, which had temporarily become invaded by the transference resistance, had been restored, although the transference itself was far from resolved (see especially Greenson 1965b). In fact, the patient clung tenaciously to her feelings of being mistreated by the therapist and, at times, would attempt to provoke such mistreatment. The next interpretive step was to try to help the patient understand the motives for her clinging to this kind of interaction in the transference. The therapist had long been aware that when the patient described much of her childhood dealings with her mother, it always centered on instances of what she felt were her mother's overly demanding and critical attitude toward her. Her usual description of her mother was of an overworked, tired, remote, and depressed woman whose attention was hard to get. The therapist felt that the patient, in the transference, was struggling to hold on to him. The patient felt she needed him, despite her feeling of being mistreated by him, in conformity with her experience as a child of having her mother's attention only when struggling with or submitting to her.

> *Therapist:* Sometimes you struggle with me because you feel that, otherwise, you will not continue to feel involved with me, which is how you have described feeling during periods when your mother seemed depressed and uninterested in you.
> *Patient:* You know, I often felt as a little girl that my mother's only interest in me was as someone to complain to or as someone to criticize and belittle. I still feel that way, sometimes.

> *Therapist:* These kinds of interactions with her may have felt like the way in which she loved you when you were a little girl, even if now you remember them in a different way.

The therapist helped the patient recognize an important reason for her perpetuation of sadomasochistic interactions, both in her outside life and now in the transference. They represented a distorted loving tie with her mother and her only way of holding on to someone she felt she needed, but who was otherwise unavailable.

Other motives for her clinging to such a seemingly painful mode of personal involvement soon surfaced. It had long been obvious that, in addition to feeling victimized by her mother, the patient powerfully identified with her mother's critical as well as suffering ways. In the transference she was always criticizing the therapist as well as suffering from his perceived selfish mistreatment of her. During one session, she was describing a particularly painful childhood memory of a friend's birthday party she was preparing to attend.

> *Patient:* I was putting on my party dress. It had a sash that tied behind me. I was too small to get it right. I remember mother smiling, watching me struggle to tie it. I started to cry. The whole time she seemed irritated at having to help me. Just as I was leaving, I remember walking down the hallway to the front door. I thought I looked beautiful in my party dress. Mother said, "We've got to lengthen that dress. It's too short." I felt crushed. I remember tearing apart my favorite doll that day. I would often break or throw away my favorite things.
> *Therapist:* So you became, in your play, like your mother, and did to your toys what she did to you.

The patient was helped to recognize her identification with her mother's sadism by this and many subsequent interpretations. It became clear that, as the patient grew older, her mother fostered this kind of identification by covertly approving of the patient's critical views of her peers and family members. Being critical, mistrustful, and easily hurt seemed to elicit her mother's approval and thus guarantee her love and interest.

> *Therapist:* For you to feel more trusting, less critical, and less hurt by me would be separating yourself from your mother, giving up her love and approval.

Here the therapist links the transference and its antecedents in a way only possible during the middle phase of treatment, after many previous interpretations about the same material. It should be noted that, in this middle phase transference interpretation, the therapist does not distinguish between past and present. The therapist might, in fact, refer back to this interpretation by noting "you can't please her and trust me," even if "pleasing" refers to the past and "trusting" to the therapeutic present. By the middle phase, such "timeless" wording of transference interpretations helps the patient to become familiar and comfortable with the continuity of past and present. Put differently, interpretations worded in this way emphasize the "timeless" nature of unconscious processes. If transference interpretations are carefully and consistently structured in this way, most patients can be observed to begin to phrase their self-observations in a similar manner, an important signal to the therapist of therapeutic movement in the transference work. It should be pointed out that this series of interventions extended over many weeks of treatment, a fact easily lost sight of in clinical case reports. The working through of a transference resistance is a long and usually laborious process. It took this patient many months before she was, in any consistent way, able to recognize the masochistic experience of her treatment as the result of her unconsciously repeating and clinging to her distorted relationship with her mother. Many other facets of both her identification with and struggles against her mother, and their continual repetition in all her other important relationships, were worked out in an interpretive way analogous to the interventions outlined here. Gradually she became less critical and more comfortable with the therapist as new issues took center stage in the treatment.

RESISTANCE TO THE TRANSFERENCE

In any ongoing psychotherapy, the therapist can expect that all-important and enduring emotional relationships dating from the patient's formative years, particularly in their conflictual aspects, will, if given sufficient time, appear in the distortions of the transference. The sequence and intensity of such transference developments will vary significantly from patient to patient and will be most complete in analysis. The foregoing is ensured by the regressive forces inherent in analytic treatments, by the therapist's efforts to facilitate transference developments, and by the pressure of unconscious conflictual material for conscious expression. Additionally, powerful forces within the patient may interfere with the emergence of transference phenomena. They need to be explored and worked through via interpretation in order for the transference to serve in the fullest possible way as a vehicle for resolution of the patient's internal difficulties. Resistance to the transference is the term used to describe the patient's efforts, usually unconscious, to avoid the emergence of transference material. Such resistance may be to specific transference elements or, in some patients, to transference in general. There are many sources of such resistance, including specific fears and conflicts associated with the particular childhood relationship; more general fears of regression, of loss of control, and of the unconscious; and problems in the therapeutic alliance. The therapist's approach to such resistances should be in keeping with the principles of interpretation of resistance outlined in Chapter 4. Two clinical examples illustrate typical interpretive approaches to resistance to the transference: one to a specific transference development, the other to the emergence of transference material in general.

The treatment of the patient described in the previous section on transference resistance included an illustrative example of work on resistance to the transference. This occurred following the working through of the patient's struggles and identification with her mother via interpretation of the sadomasochistic resistance, which was the transference reenactment of this relationship. The therapist had reason to expect that, following what seemed to be at least a partial resolution of some of the patient's conflicts in this area, transference material concerning the patient's relationship to her father would begin to emerge. The therapist knew from an early information-gathering phase of the treatment, during which the patient somewhat blandly recounted the history of her relationship with both her parents, that her childhood attachment to her father was relatively distant. Furthermore, there was evidence that the patient's mother did little to foster this relationship and, in fact, resented any warmth the father showed toward the patient. A vague suggestion of sexual forbiddenness accompanied the patient's early description of her episodic childhood interactions with her father.

The working through of stormy struggles in the maternal transference ushered in a period of relative calm in the therapy. To some extent, this was a welcome development, a chance for more cooperative work. The therapist gradually became aware of a sense of blandness and distance in the way the patient responded to him. The patient also seemed to be overly careful in her relationship to him. The therapist wondered whether this represented the patient's conscious efforts to avoid further sadomasochistic struggles with the therapist, in a sense representing a positive change in the patient resulting from the previous period of work on these difficulties. He also wondered whether the blandness reflected the patient's often distant relationship with her father. Yet the historical material indicated that the patient, although not consistently close to or affectionate with her father, had nonetheless felt that he loved her and had a positive influence on her. She had reported a longing for more involvement with him.

Following a week-long hiatus in the treatment, while the therapist was out of town, the patient seemed happy to see him and smiled at him as she entered the office.

Patient: Boy, I missed you. I mean, I really missed the sessions.

The patient seemed anxious about her opening comment and, after a moment, began to fill the therapist in on the events of the previous week, particularly emphasizing the ways she felt her family had mistreated her. The therapist wondered whether the material about being mistreated was a displacement of her feelings of being mistreated by him. Absent from her report was any indication of awareness that she had had at least some active role in provoking the mistreatment by her family, a seeming retreat from her previous therapeutic gains. Most striking to the therapist was the almost automatic initiation of masochistic complaints following her telling him that she had missed him, anxiously "neutralized" to missing the sessions.

Therapist: You began by telling me that you missed me, and then felt obliged to change this to missing the sessions as though missing me was somehow unacceptable.
Patient: It is the sessions. I don't really even know you. This relationship is so strange. It's businesslike.
Therapist: You became anxious about making your feelings sound more personal than businesslike.
Patient: I did feel funny about it. I like to keep this very businesslike. When I said I missed you, I thought, "I don't want to sound like I'm coming on to him."

There followed the gradual revelation of the patient's struggles to hold back her affectionate and sexual feelings and fantasies about the therapist, to keep things businesslike. She reported that when she did acknowledge, to herself, such feelings, she felt anxious, uncomfortable, and very critical of herself. Her associations led to her mother's jealous and accusatory responses to her tender moments with her father. The patient remembered that her mother always characterized any openly affectionate interactions with her father in a vaguely unsavory way that made her feel guilty and frightened. She remarked that, even as an adult, she became uncomfortable when greeting her father with a kiss.

> *Therapist:* When you told me you missed me, you felt as though your mother was watching you act seductively toward me.
> *Patient:* Yes. I especially remember my mother yelling at me for letting my father see me in the bath as a little girl. I've never forgotten that.

The patient began a phase of work that centered around her longed-for loving attachment to her father, memories of her occasional warm moments with him, and guilt about the sexual wishes and feelings associated with these memories. There was a great deal of material about her adult difficulty in being openly seductive and erotic with men, unless it was absolutely clear that they had approached her first. In the transference, work on this material led to her greater freedom in feeling loving, seductive, or generally less "business-like" in her relations with the therapist. It became clear that she had struggled to keep this aspect of the transference from materializing earlier. Her memories centered on her mother's demands that she see the father in the same devalued way her mother viewed him. She recalled her growing feeling as a child that her father did, in fact, prefer her to her constantly complaining, critical mother. She remembered, as well, her guilty struggles over her sexual attraction to her father, which her mother continually hinted might at any moment lead to some active incestuous conclusion. Thus the resistance to the positive paternal transference was understood and worked through. A more adequate separation from the powerful masochistic identification with her mother was made possible as the therapist, in the transference, became an available safe new object for the patient in a way her father had never been.

In this example, the resistance to the positive paternal transference, as well as this transference itself, once it did emerge, were both reenactments of childhood events. This illustrates the fact that all resistance, in this case the resistance to the transference, itself reflects important aspects of the patient's psychic equilibrium, often with very significant developmental referents that must be explored along with the material being resisted, a point emphasized in Chapter 4. With regard to the concept of resistance to the transference, one might say such resistance is part of, as well as an avoidance of, the transference, and both aspects should be explored and interpreted.

A second kind of resistance to the transference is resistance to transference responses in general. For the majority of patients with neurotic disorders, transference phenomena develop slowly and gain in intensity as therapy proceeds. The patient must begin to feel that the treatment situation is a safe place to allow the regressive process that allows the fullest development of transference. The therapist must become an important and reliable ally to the patient in his struggle to gain relief from his difficulties. Transference for certain patients stirs up powerful fears of loss of control, of irreversible or unmanageable regression, or of intolerable closeness and dependence on the therapist. Thus the transference must be avoided, often by a hypervigilant attention to being clear, fair, realistic, and "adult." When such patients perceive the emergence of intensely emotional attitudes toward the therapist, they frequently interpret their own behavior in ways that, although superficially insightful, with accurate historical parallels, are in fact designed to undo, negate, isolate, and intellectualize developments in transference. The therapist's first interpretive task is to avoid joining the patient in this way of resisting the transference by becoming too absorbed in premature, intellectualizing interpretations. Rather, the therapist needs to call the patient's attention to the way in which he seems intent on maintaining a certain here-and-now, adult, "rational" quality in his relationship with the therapist. In keeping with the general suggestions for interpretation of resistance outlined in Chapter 4, this must be done in a manner that recognizes that the patient values his avoidance of "irrationality," based upon conscious as well as unconscious fears of giving in to the regressive pull of the transference. These fears must be brought to light and interpreted in order to overcome the resistance. Efforts to encourage or induce transference phenomena, by means other than the conditions already inherent in the treatment situation, are bound to be unproductive, as are most efforts designed to bypass resistances rather than analyze them. It should also be mentioned that intense resistance to transference development may signal otherwise less obvious severe pathology, often of a paranoid type, which might suggest a rethinking of the advisability of pursuing an uncovering, analytic approach with the patient. However, this is neither regularly the case, nor should it be taken to mean that the presence of paranoid traits per se contraindicates analytic treatments.

> The patient, a divorced psychologist in his mid-fifties, sought treatment because of depression, decreased interest and productivity in his work, and problems in his social and work relationships. Although psychologically sophisticated, he seemed unaware of the manner in which he used this knowledge in a defensive way in treatment. He was conscious of many troublesome obsessional character traits and wished help in modifying them.
> During the first few months of treatment, the therapist learned a great deal about the patient's upbringing in a somewhat rigid Catholic family dominated by his parents' unhappy marriage and constant bickering. His father was prone to temper outbursts, which intimidated the family and frightened the patient as a small child. The patient recalled many struggles with both his parents over rules and prohibitions, many of which he felt were arbitrary and unfair. Frequently these struggles led to his having temper

tantrums, for which he was severely punished. As a grade-school child, he had difficulty with peers due to temper outbursts, which often led to fist fights. Although these ended as he entered adolescence, his bad temper remained part of the family lore and was frequently mentioned at family gatherings. As an adult, he was professionally successful, but had few friends. He had a short-lived marriage in his mid-twenties and was unhappy and lonely most of the time. He felt better just being in treatment and consciously attempted to cooperate with the free association process and other aspects of the therapy.

The therapist noted that the patient's attitude toward him had a somewhat bland and distant quality, occasionally interrupted by the patient's intellectualized report of some feeling or fantasy involving the therapist, the mention of which was often removed in time from its occurrence. The therapist continually wondered what particular parental role the patient might be casting him in, but no evidence of any lasting development of transference was detectable. The therapist did not feel that the patient was oblivious of him in the way certain narcissistic patients are, nor did he feel that the patient was hiding feelings about him. Gradually it became clear that the patient was defending himself against the development of any transference feelings by emphasizing his rational cooperativeness. He carefully watched for any sign of departure from this attitude, which, if it did occur, was quickly lifted to the intellectual realm where its exploration rendered it lifeless. The therapist felt the treatment, although seemingly helpful to the patient in terms of a partial lifting of his depressed mood, had little chance of having any lasting impact on the patient's character structure unless the resistance to the transference could be overcome.

During one particular session, the patient mentioned that he would have to miss a session the following week due to a business trip.

Patient: I suppose I'll have some feeling about missing.
Therapist: You seem uncertain about that.
Patient: Well, anyway, it's a trip I have to take. No choice about it.

Therapist: I think your comment about supposing you'll have some feeling about missing refers to your recognition that we would expect that the emotional bond between us should be something we can see and talk about. Yet we rarely do.

Patient: You know, I've known many people in therapy and they have all sorts of exaggerated, crazy ideas about their therapists. It's all they can talk about sometimes. It's not like that here. I'm not like that.

Therapist: I have the impression that you keep any less sensible, unrealistic, perhaps even childish feelings about me out of your own awareness. When they occasionally do occur, you focus all your attention on understanding them in a way that is mostly designed to put an end to them.

Here the therapist interprets, in a general way, the patient's efforts to avoid the therapeutic regression that would result in the emergence of transference phenomena. His interpretation is in response to the patient's own observation about the nature of his predicted response to missing a session, which hints at some recognition, on the patient's part, that something is not quite right in his emotional responsiveness in the treatment. The therapist emphasizes that the patient seems to be avoiding something. Although no dramatic change was forthcoming, the therapist now made a point of calling the patient's attention to his immediately intellectualizing any feelings the therapist or the treatment stirred up in him. The therapist noted again and again how the patient turned feeling into thought, as if letting the feeling go on too long was something the patient felt he must avoid. The therapist also encouraged the patient to explore what he meant by other patients having "exaggerated, crazy ideas about their therapists." The patient described his own discomfort upon observing signs of what were obvious transference manifestations in people he knew who were in therapy. The patient's associations to this discomfort led to material about his temper outbursts as a child and to his adult discomfort at hearing about them at family gatherings.

> *Therapist:* We can surmise that you have set yourself the task of unconsciously avoiding ever letting your feelings get that out of control again because it was so frightening and subsequently embarrassing to you. In your relationship with me, this takes the form of being careful to always be reasonable and rational.

This interpretation led the patient to recall, in even more detail, his tantrums as a child, his struggles against having them, his fears of retaliation, his fears of his father's tantrums, and the gradual restriction of his emotionality, which could at least be partially understood as the outcome of these conflicts. With this interpretive work, a slowly evolving loosening of his rigid control over conscious awareness of feeling states occurred and, concomitantly, transference elements began to emerge with greater regularity and freedom.

This sequence of interpretations took many months. It was elicited by emphasizing the patient's own observation, his supposition that he would respond to not seeing the therapist with some feeling, an indirect commentary by the patient on his recognition of some conflict about such feelings. In patiently and attentively waiting for such an opportunity, the therapist could then interpret in a way that included the patient's self-observation, a general principle of interpretation worth reemphasizing. Subsequent interpretation focused on the resistance, avoidance of spontaneous emotion and regression through intellectualization and defensive rationality, reasonableness, and cooperativeness. This required much repetition until the patient became familiar with an aspect of himself of which he was relatively unaware due to its automatic nature—its structuralization as part of his character. Next the therapist compared the patient's discomfort with the alternative way of reacting the patient observed in others, which eventually led to an exploration of the unconscious roots of this discomfort in his childhood conflicts over anger and loss of control. This sequential interpretive approach to resistance, described in Chapter 4, eventually led to a gradual resolution of this patient's resistance to the transference in a manner that more direct exhortation or encouragement of transference material could never have accomplished. The therapist emphasized, in his interpretations, the patient's need for control of his anger as a child, in view of his fears about his parents' far from optimal responses to his tantrums. These included openly belittling him, severely punishing him, and demanding rigid control from him, all made necessary by their own character pathology. The therapist took care not to belittle the patient over his need for control. He helped him to see that this control was only necessary so long as he saw the therapeutic relationship as an extension or new version of the family situation as he remembered it as a child. His fears of retaliation and humiliation were carefully exposed and clarified as a prerequisite for his allowing himself to experience the freedom, security, and trust necessary for the therapeutic regression that permits the development of transference. In general, one could say that the patient's resistance to transference was a reenactment of his compliant, obedient, and fearful submission to his parents, illustrating the thesis that resistances usually express, in some way, the very mental content they are designed to ward off. For this reason, the interpretive approach described focuses on the resistance itself, rather than on attempting to bypass it in hopes of encouraging those transference developments the resistance wards off. As might be expected, each new transference development required a further working through of the above interpretations in light of the new material brought out as the work continued.

_____ Transference Resolution _____

Why does a patient give up a transference attitude and what role does interpretation have in facilitating this process? In general, we can say that a transference attitude is given up when its origins in old conflicts are made conscious and when the distortions that interfered with a satisfactory resolution of these conflicts are examined in a new light that favors a more adaptive outcome than was possible in the past. Interpretation is the means by which these old conflicts and the distortions associated with them are made conscious and understandable to the patient. On the other hand, interpretations specifically designed to resolve transferences in the sense of being directed toward ending transference attitudes are necessary and desirable only under special circumstances. Many of the issues surrounding such instances will be discussed in Chapter 8. Here, some general principles of interpretation relative to transference resolution not directly related to termination issues will be emphasized.

In an analytic treatment that extends over any period of time, the therapist can expect a series of transference distortions representing the patient's sequentially changing relationships with the important figures of his childhood. In most cases, these transferences will evolve and change as the underlying memories, fantasies, distortions, and conflicts come to the surface and are explored and understood. The therapist's attitude toward these distortions, as shown by the way the patient interacts with him, should be one of interest, patience, and acceptance, based on the recognition of the value of these distortions in revitalizing the patient's unconscious conflicts, particularly those that reflect the problems of childhood. The therapist's expectation should be that various transferences will resolve themselves when the underlying conflicts that, in a sense, drive or fuel them are understood and modified. When a particular transference attitude does not yield in the face of an interpretive approach to its underlying conflicts and distortions, the therapist must ask himself certain questions. Is the current understanding of the transference correct or complete? For example, is a male patient's overly compliant and obedient transference attitude toward the therapist a reenactment of his fearful retreat from his competitive attitude toward his violence-prone father? Or does it also represent a more hidden homosexual seduction of the therapist as father, which also needs to be explored and interpreted before the transference will yield?

Another possibility to be considered is whether the interpretations of a particular attitude are, in fact, correct and relatively complete in terms of the material from the past that they represent but that, in some not readily apparent way, the therapist's response to the transference sufficiently gratifies the unconscious wishes that are part of the underlying conflict the patient clings to the transference. For example, a patient's sadomasochistic transference struggles may be irritating enough so that the therapist's subtle annoyance, either in the way he interprets the transference or responds to a prolongation of such struggles, may be such that the continued gratification of the patient's sadomasochistic wishes serves to maintain the transference even after its adequate interpretation. This is a common countertransference problem with certain patients and needs to be carefully watched for by the therapist.

A further instance of difficulty in the resolution of the transference occurs when a particular transference becomes a resistance to the emergence of some other transference paradigm. This requires interpretation beyond the elucidation of the transference itself. The transference has become a way of warding off or resisting other material, a phenomenon that can be considered a change in function of the transference from reliving aspects of one conflictual relationship to avoiding another. As with most resistances, there is important content in the resistance itself; it often turns out that clinging to the particular relationship revived in the transference served a similar avoidance function in the patient's past. Thus, interpretation of this form of difficulty in transference resolution should include a search for historical antecedents of hanging on to someone to avoid another frightening or, in some other way, troublesome object tie.

In summary, several types of problems in transference resolution have been described. In principle, these should be handled as other resistances to the natural exposure of unconscious material, the expectation being that no coercive measures are required to "resolve" transference. It must be understood that work on a particular form of the transference may take months or even years, especially when the particular transference material concerns central conflicts and identifications in the patient that have become part of the patient's character structure. Transference phenomena continue throughout analytic treatments and may not be totally resolved even at the end of a lengthy analysis, an issue discussed further in Chapter 8 on termination interpretations.

Suggested Readings

Bird, B. (1972). Notes on transference: Universal phenomenon and hardest part of analysis. *Journal of the American Psychoanalytic Association* 20:267–301.

> This paper offers a particularly illuminating look at the concepts of the transference, transference neurosis, negative transference, negative therapeutic reaction, and countertransference. The author avoids jargon and is evocative, provocative, and casts the struggle, which in analytic treatments eventually surfaces in the transference relationship in dramatic, compelling terms. He brings life to and accurately portrays the difficult task of resolving the transference neurosis, particularly its negative, hostile, destructive elements. The author also examines transference as an ego function and speculates on its role in other ego activities.

Daniels, R. S. (1969). Some early manifestations of transference. *Journal of the American Psychoanalytic Association* 17:995–1014.

> This paper is a good summary of the important issues to be considered in formulating interpretations during the early phase of treatment. It describes early transference manifestations and their management in three illustrative clinical vignettes.

Freud, S. (1912a). The dynamics of transference. *Standard Edition* 12:99–108.

—— (1915). Observations on transference—love. *Standard Edition* 12:159–171.

> These two papers, taken together, summarize Freud's view of the centrality of the interpretation of transference to the therapeutic

action of psychoanalysis. Freud examines the nature of transference, its here-and-now and repetition of the past aspects, its
impact on the analyst, and its relationship to the patient's neurosis. Particularly important are his comments about the "reality"
of the transference and the analyst's correct response to it.

Gill, M. M., and Muslin, H. L. (1976). Early interpretation of transference. *Journal of the American Psychoanalytic Association*
24:779–794.

The authors argue for making early transference interpretations,
based upon here-and-now interactions in the treatment, without
being bound by the need to include genetic reconstructions, the
data for which would usually be unavailable early in treatment,
or by the dictum that the transference must become a resistance
before it is interpreted. They trace this latter viewpoint to an
early stage in the development of technique when it was mistakenly thought that a patient was free of transference resistance
if he was free associating readily. They offer examples of early
transference interpretations in the course of a brief clinical
vignette.

Gill, M. M. (1979). The analysis of the transference. *Journal of the
American Psychoanalytic Association Suppl.* 27:263–289.

This paper is a good summary of the author's views regarding the
centrality of transference interpretation to the analytic process.
The relationship between transference and resistance is examined
and suggestions are made about the best interpretive approach to
the transference resistances. Gill believes the major work in
resolving the transference takes place in the present, with genetic
transference interpretations playing a lesser role and following
naturally from work on resistances in the transference as they
take place in the here-and-now. The author's views on the nature
of interpretive work on the transference are controversial in
psychoanalytic circles but are worthwhile for study, due to their
clarity and explicitness.

Greenacre, P. (1954). The role of transference. *Journal of the
American Psychoanalytic Association* 2:671–684.

The author characterizes "a firm basic transference" derived from
the mother–child relationship. To this is added a reactivation of
past emotional attitudes in the patient induced by the nonpartici-
pation of the analyst in a personal way, which creates a "tilted"
emotional relationship. The therapist's anonymity is stressed.
The author contrasts the relative importance of this basic positive transference and the more regressively distorting transfer-

ence reactions that develop in response to the therapist's remaining in the background. The author regards the latter, fullest development of the transference and its interpretation as crucial to the psychoanalytic method. Her paper, frequently cited as representing the most "classical" of positions about transference, argues against attempts to manipulate the transference, to shorten analysis by coercively inducing only partial transference developments, and to undermine the importance of the analyst's relative anonymity, neutrality, and objectivity in protecting the transference from "contamination" and thus interfering with the usefulness of its fullest development and interpretation.

Greenson, R. R., and Wexler, M. (1969). The non-transference relationship in the psychoanalytic situation. *International Journal of Psycho-Analysis* 50:27–39.

In this work, the authors examine the non-transference or "real" relationship between the patient and therapist in its interaction with the development of transference distortions. They argue for attention to the humanity of the therapist in his dealings with the patient, and explore the manner in which the patient's accurate perceptions of "real" characteristics and behaviors of the therapist contribute to the transference. The authors contrast the real relationship with an exclusive focus on interpretation. They also advocate attending to the patient's reality attributes, his strengths, and his realistic reactions. This is a valuable and interesting paper to read, although many critics view the separation of the therapeutic relationship into "real," "working," and transference parts as artificial and misleading.

Macalpine, I. (1950). The development of the transference. *Psychoanalytic Quarterly* 19:501–539.

This paper is particularly useful in its emphasis on the ways that the analytic environment, a "rigid infantile setting," requires an adaptive regression by the patient that results in the analytic transference in a "transference-ready" patient. This view is contrasted with the more usual view of transference as arising spontaneously from within the patient. Read in conjunction with other, more "classical" views about transference, a more balanced position about the etiology of transference phenomena can be formulated to allow interpretations of transference that recognize the contributions of the therapist, the setting, and unconscious processes in the patient to the transference. [See especially Gill (1979) for another viewpoint, which also emphasizes the analyst's contributions to the transference that should be acknowledged in interpretive interventions.]

Orr, D. W. (1954). Transference and countertransference: A historical survey. *Journal of the American Psychoanalytic Association* 2:621–670.

> This paper is a useful and often cited historical review of the various meanings ascribed to the terms transference and countertransference within the classical psychoanalytic literature up to the time of its writing. It also describes differing viewpoints about the technical handling of these phenomena. The paper is particularly useful in outlining the broad areas of disagreement among analysts about what constitutes countertransference.

6

Countertransference Interpretations

The issue of countertransference interpretation is an un-settled one among psychoanalytic therapists. Whereas there is general agreement that transference interpretation is an integral part of any analytic treatment and that failure to interpret the transference in a timely and appropriate man-ner interferes with the progress of the therapy, management of the countertransference, and its integration into treatment technique, varies widely among therapists. This lack of clarity is partly due to the different meanings ascribed to the term countertransference within the literature. Although most experienced therapists agree that the countertransfer-ence, regardless of how it is defined, is at times a source of useful information about the patient and the progress of the treatment, whether and how to introduce this information into the treatment process via interpretation remains an area of dispute and widely varying clinical practice.

_____ The Meanings of Countertransference _____

The term countertransference was one Freud rarely used and never explored in a systematic manner that might have led to a generally psychoanalytic definition. Perhaps this partly explains the subsequent confusion surrounding the term's later usage by psychoanalytic writers and teachers. Furthermore, because, from its inception, the term implied a negative, unwanted, and even psychopathological process in the therapist, the exploration of countertransference in one's own work, and especially with colleagues and in the literature, lagged behind investigations of other therapeutic issues. When countertransference finally did become an area of active investigation and discussion, its usage reflected the different theoretical and clinical perspectives of widely divergent psychoanalytic groups, which made it difficult to integrate their contributions. In its broadest definition, countertransference refers to all those feelings stirred up in the therapist by the patient. In its narrowest usage, countertransference refers to the therapist's specific unconscious reactions to the patient's transference. For some, the term applies only to untherapeutic, unconsciously determined, neurotic attitudes of the therapist toward the patient, either in response to the patient's specific transference provocations or in response to the patient generally. Other investigators speak of the countertransference as occurring when the patient becomes the object of feelings in the therapist that are remnants of unresolved conflicts with important people from the therapist's past, countertransference here roughly meaning the therapist's transference to the patient. Another group of therapists, following the lead of a group of British psychoanalysts, equates countertransference with unconscious perceptiveness, the way in which the therapist's unconscious processes respond to and thus provide valuable clues about corresponding or parallel unconscious processes in the patient, especially during periods of troubled verbal communication during the treatment. With this broad a range of meanings, countertransference as a clinical concept loses the precision and clarity necessary for careful study and the development of a cohesive set of guidelines for formulating interpretations of countertransference phenomena.

In approaching this thorny area of clinical theory, it seems reasonable to differentiate at least two broad classes of phenomena that have, at one time or another, been described as countertransference. The first group includes those phenomena encompassed by definitions that describe all the therapist's emotional reactions to the patient, including the therapist's unconscious perceptions, as countertransference. The second group includes those situations in which unconscious processes in the therapist interfere with his ability to understand and be helpful to the patient. The former broad category of meanings really refers to the manner in which the therapist comes to emotionally know the patient via the unconscious communications and mutual responsiveness that ordinarily develop in any intimate relationship and to which the therapist, by virtue of his training, experience, objectivity, and focused attention, is acutely sensitive. This source of information about the patient should not be viewed as countertransference along with those phenomena in the second group, if the term countertransference is to be of practical value to the clinician. The latter group, which is characterized by the sometimes transient and, at other times, more lasting interference of unconscious processes in the therapist with his capacity to understand and therefore be therapeutic, is more appropriately described as countertransference only to the extent it represents at least a temporary obstacle to progress in the therapeutic work requiring some remedial activity on the therapist's part. Inevitably some overlap between these groups occurs, but a relatively clear distinction is usually possible. The subsequent discussion of countertransference interpretation refers to this latter group, although many of the recommendations regarding interpretive technique apply to the former group of phenomena as well.

_____ Countertransference and Interpretation _____

A pivotal issue in the debate about countertransference
interpretation is the therapist's relative anonymity, a concept that requires clarification in order to avoid some common misconceptions and errors in technique. Anonymity is
an unfortunate choice of terms to describe the therapist's
position in the patient's emotional life during treatment. The
therapist is neither an anonymous stranger nor a mirror that
reflects the patient's inner world during therapy. The mirror
metaphor (Freud 1912b) is useful in describing how the distortions of the patient are made more easily distinguishable
and available for interpretive work if the therapist's personal life, his values, and his preferences are kept in the
background, yet it gives an emotionally inaccurate picture
of what the therapist's role should be. The therapist must
become a trusted ally in the patient's quest for relief from
his problems, someone the patient will come to know a good
deal about in terms of the therapist's way of understanding
mental life. Furthermore, the patient will, over time, learn
about the therapist's idiosyncrasies, his tolerance for frustration, his prejudices, and his areas of conflict, as these are
revealed in his handling of the patient's often less than
cooperative behavior, uncomfortable moments in the therapeutic relationship, money matters, appointment changes,
and the other everyday stresses that are part of the work of
treatment. What anonymity should mean is that the therapist will make every effort to maintain the focus on the
patient's life and problems. He will avoid introducing ex-
traneous personal information that will divert the patient's
attention or obscure the patient's inevitable transference
distortions of the therapist. He will keep his own value
judgments, moral attitudes, prejudices, and areas of special
interest in the background, so that the patient will feel as
free as possible to explore his inner life in a way that need not
be tailored to the therapist's personal needs or preferences.

Inevitably, during the course of the therapeutic work,
and particularly in response to the patient's regressive trans-

ference demands and provocations, the therapist will discover that he has difficulty in functioning in his usual
objective, non-anxious, neutral, reflective, and relatively
anonymous manner. He may feel tempted to directly or indirectly scold the patient, he may unnecessarily reveal some
personal information about himself, he may miss some otherwise easily recognizable theme in the material, he may interpret to punish rather than to elucidate, he may forget a
session, or he may in a myriad of other ways depart from his
usual manner of working. Often it is only after the fact that
the therapist will realize that he has been having difficulty.
Sometimes the patient will make him aware of it. Especially
during training, a supervisor may be the one to point out a
problem. These problems may be the result of something a
particular patient is stirring up in the therapist or may
represent an intrusion of problems the therapist is having or
has had in his personal life into his work with certain patients. All these difficulties have been described as countertransference by one or another writer. Although it is beyond
the scope of this discussion to categorize and outline distin-
guishing characteristics of all the different kinds of countertransference problems that may be encountered, it is worth
mentioning that there are very significant differences that
need to be taken into account by the therapist in order that
they are correctly handled.

Countertransference phenomena provide valuable information about the patient, and particularly with seriously
disturbed patients, may be among the most significant sources
of data during certain periods of the treatment. Yet it should
be made clear that, at least initially, countertransference as
the term is being used here interferes with understanding
and proper management of the treatment. The therapist must
work hard, often with the help of a supervisor or colleague,
to use his difficulty as a source of information as well as to
overcome the interference it causes in his handling of the
clinical work. The broad category of phenomena that defines
as countertransference the full range of feelings and unconscious perceptions stirred up in the therapist by the patient

gives the false impression that countertransference is an ongoing, easily available source of data for interpretation and that such interpretations constitute a regular part of the work. Countertransference as it is used here is a more limited phenomenon, one that presumably occurs only occasionally and one that requires special handling in order to serve as the basis for interpretation.

Countertransference interpretations should be designed to use the information about the patient the therapist's scrutiny of his own difficulty has revealed, while not burdening the patient with unnecessary material about the therapist's mental processes. Put differently, countertransference interpretations should be made within the context of the therapist's relative anonymity and neutrality. Failure to make interpretations in such a manner, although sanctioned by some writers, tends to compound countertransference difficulties and minimizes the usefulness of such interpretations. In a sense, the term countertransference interpretation is a misnomer. There need not be interpretations that elucidate for the patient the nature and scope of the therapist's countertransference difficulties. Countertransference interpretations are really interpretations that use the information relevant to the patient revealed to the therapist in his self-scrutiny of his temporary difficulty in the therapeutic process. Because patients are often, but not always, aware of such difficulties, such interpretations may indirectly reveal or acknowledge the presence of countertransference, but their emphasis must be on the patient. Confessional and defensive explanatory interventions by the therapist are counterproductive and should be avoided. It is sometimes argued that not to acknowledge or explain an error, in this case, one due to countertransference, creates turmoil in the patient, due to the therapist's perceived defensiveness. However, it is possible to interpret with regard to such errors in a way that avoids defensiveness as well as unnecessary self-revelation, to further the patient's self-awareness.

Deciding when to interpret countertransference issues requires careful attention to the therapist's own response to his awareness of having had some problem. Many, perhaps most, minor countertransference difficulties are discovered and resolved by the therapist without an error of any significance having been made and without the patient's being aware of the therapist's turmoil. In such instances, it is usually possible for the therapist to decide without too much difficulty how to use any information about the patient derived from an understanding of the countertransference. In most instances, no interpretive intervention is required, and the therapist should take care not to guiltily call unnecessary attention to the countertransference. Much more difficult are instances in which the therapist's countertransference appears to have resulted in an untherapeutic exchange or error the patient has recognized. What makes many of these incidents difficult to manage and interpret is the fact that they occur in response to intense transference provocation by the patient. For example, a superficially compliant and respectful, but subtly disparaging patient may provoke the therapist to make an intervention the therapist recognizes is more retaliatory than elucidating. The patient responds by feeling unfairly attacked. What makes such a situation difficult is that the patient is recreating an object relationship in which the therapist is provoked into playing one of the roles once played by an important person in the patient's past, or by the patient himself. The patient will experience the therapist's responses in terms of the unconscious transference configuration. Thus in this example, the patient might have felt unfairly attacked even by a neutral, objective response from the therapist. It is often very difficult to be certain whether the patient's response to the therapist is related to the latter's countertransference or to the patient's transference distortion of him. The more intense the provocation, the more likely any activity or even inactivity by the therapist will be seen by the patient in a way that conforms to his unconscious recreation of the past. Thus, the therapist should be careful that his awareness of having been provoked and the patient's complaint about being mistreated, although they may temporally coincide, do not necessarily indicate that the patient has recognized a countertransference reaction in the therapist. Confessional interpretations at such times make it more difficult for the patient to use subsequent interpretations about the transference meanings of the provoking behavior because they unnecessarily emphasize the therapist's "real" responses in the here-and-now. Nor is it always countertransference to be provoked. The image of the imperturbable analyst has always been exaggerated, and some have even argued that the patient needs, under certain circumstances, to be able to create countertransference disturbances in the therapist (Tower 1956). What is important is that the therapist be aware of his emotional responsiveness to the patient's transference distortions and search carefully for his own possible contributions to difficulties in the progress of the therapeutic work that may result from such distortions.

> The patient, a woman in her mid-forties came for analytic treatment because of marital difficulties and troublesome relationships with her adolescent children. During the first few months of her treatment, she complained ever more openly and bitterly about the way her husband constantly criticized her. She spoke of her ambivalence about divorcing him. She reported feeling wounded and angry after most of her interactions with him. As she gradually filled in a picture of her childhood, it became clear that her relationship with her mother also was characterized by the latter's critical attitude toward her, at least as the patient remembered it. The patient's relationship toward the therapist seemed anxiously friendly, somewhat ingratiating, and always forced and uncomfortable.
>   The therapist felt that the treatment was going along fairly well and reported on the progress of the case to his supervisor. On several occasions, the supervisor wondered why the therapist had not interpreted certain fairly obvious themes in the material. Although the therapist had no ready explanation and the supervisor felt there would be many other opportunities to interpret the same material, the therapist did acknowledge that, for reasons unclear to

him, he was particularly quiet and cautious in his interventions with this patient.

On one particular occasion, the patient was describing an incident in which it was clear that the patient was unconsciously setting up her teenage son to criticize her unfairly. As the therapist began to say something about this, he became aware that he was having an unusually difficult time finding a good way of describing something quite simple. His interpretation was overly long, vague, and unnatural-sounding. The patient listened, then replied that she was not sure what the therapist meant. The therapist repeated in more abbreviated form, his observation, to which the patient replied, "Now I see what you mean."

The therapist wondered to himself why he had been so vague. He knew from past experience that when he made long-winded interpretations, he was conflicted in some way about what he was saying. He remembered an incident many years earlier during his training, when, following a circuitous interpretation to a group, a patient had replied, "It's OK, Doc; say it so we can understand it; we can take it." During the session that followed the current vague and lengthy interpretation, the patient referred back to the therapist's intervention by noting, "Your comment yesterday sliced right through my troubles with Mike."

The therapist was immediately struck by the aggressive way the patient characterized what he thought had been a very neutrally presented observation. Almost simultaneously he remembered several other instances in which this patient had in other sessions referred back to a previously made intervention using terms like "cutting," "sharp," "pointed," and "as you made me painfully aware." The therapist now recognized that his word-finding difficulty was the result of the patient's turning his interpretations into painful attacks that hurt her. This always occurred or at least was made known to him after the fact, the patient never immediately responding to an interpretation in a way that indicated that she felt wounded. The therapist now realized, as well, that the reason he said so little to the patient, an observation also made by the supervisor, was to avoid feeling guilty about hurting her. He recognized an element of a more longstanding difficulty in himself with

regard to aggression that this patient's masochistic transference repetition had activated.

In this instance, the countertransference revealed to the
therapist the way in which the patient was using insight
for the purpose of feeling hurt, in keeping with her sadomasochistic character pathology.

Therapist: Have you noticed how you often describe my
comments to you with words like "sharp," "cutting,"
"slicing," and "painful"? Emphasizing to yourself the pain
in what I say makes it difficult to use what I say in a way
that helps you understand yourself.

The therapist's interpretation focuses on the patient's
masochism and does not mention the countertransference
difficulty that helped him to recognize how her libidiniza-
tion of insight was interfering with the progress of the work.
He avoided any mention of how her hurt response to his
interventions had stirred up conflicts in him about being
"too hurtful," resulting in his withholding interpretations.
To do so would have complicated the interpretation unnecessarily. The patient most probably was unaware of the therapist's countertransference difficulty that produced his initially lengthy, vague observation, as well as his reluctance
to make interpretations. Although it might be argued that
such patients are particularly sensitive to conflicts over
aggression in others, and might therefore unconsciously
recognize the therapist's discomfort, little would have been
gained by the therapist's revealing that the patient's masochism was making him feel guilty that his interpretations
might be hurting her. The interpretation he did make remained simple and clear and focused on the patient's problems.

This same patient was able to stir up similar conflicts in
the therapist over the boundaries of the therapeutic hour.
During a particular period in the treatment, the patient was
having difficulty speaking freely and spontaneously during
her sessions. She was depressed and greatly distressed by

the relative lack of material in the sessions and by the long painful silences. The work at the time centered on her parents' empty marriage and her mother's frequent depressions and neglect of her as a child. A pattern began to develop in which the patient had difficulty talking during most of each hour. Often, with the therapist's help and indirect encouragement, the patient began to speak more freely, frequently with great emotion, just as the sessions drew to a close. The therapist found himself reluctant to say time was up, despite his usually careful attention to considerations of time. He would let the patient run over the hour, which made him late for his next appointment. When the therapist realized that the patient was making him feel guilty about "cutting her off," he became angry with himself. He remembered how the patient often responded to the end of the session in a somewhat dejected and injured way, resignedly collecting her things and trudging out of his office looking like a beaten woman. He recalled how, months earlier, a colleague in an adjoining office, upon seeing the patient's dejected departure from the therapist's office, had jokingly asked, "what are you doing to that poor woman?" During the next session, the patient, as was her custom, came to the end of the hour in the midst of a heart-wrenching account of how, as a small child, she had on one occasion feared her mother had been killed when she did not return home from work as usual. The patient, waiting alone, had heard a distant siren, which she fantasized was an ambulance carrying away her mother. The therapist, angry about feeling uncomfortable session after session about ending the hour and in fact several times departing from his usual careful attention to promptness, abruptly interrupted the patient in mid-sentence and announced that time was up. The patient was aware of the therapist's abruptness and discomfort.

Patient: I feel like you're angry at me for complaining so much. You have always let me finish, even if it meant going over. Now it feels like you're throwing me out.
Therapist: Throwing you out?
Patient: Well, that's what it feels like. Time is up, so get out.

> *Therapist:* It has been difficult lately for us to stop without its seeming as though you were being cut off.
> *Patient:* You know how hard it has been lately for me to get started in here.
> *Therapist:* I have noticed that, in our recent sessions, you regularly arrive at the end of our time right in the middle of emotionally intense material. This is a way in which you unconsciously arrange to feel hurt and cut-off, similar to other instances we have uncovered.

In this example, the therapist again became caught up in the patient's sadomasochistic struggles with hurting and being hurt. This time his countertransference resulted in errors in technique that were obvious to the patient and led to a confrontation, a not uncommon occurrence with such patients. The therapist, after recognizing what was happening, made an interpretation that, although acknowledging the difficulty, did not burden the patient with his anger and guilt. He called the patient's attention to her active, but unconscious role in perpetuating her hurt feelings, an area of work with which the patient was familiar and which was at the root of the incident in question. To have revealed more about his own countertransference problems would have embroiled the patient further in those kinds of sadomasochistic struggles that gratify such patients and interfere with their becoming more objectively aware of their own unconscious initiation of the painful events in their lives.

As might be expected, during the next session, the patient returned to what she correctly perceived as the therapist's anger at her.

> *Patient:* I could tell you really were angry with me, no matter what you say.
> *Therapist:* You seem drawn toward focusing on what you felt were my feelings, at the expense of examining your own role in what occurred. It must be difficult for you to explore the possibility that you have some role in those painful experiences that feel to you as though they are inflicted on you by others.

Here the therapist holds firm to his interpretive focus on the patient's active role in her painful life, an important, but difficult position to maintain, following a countertransference error. Yet for the therapist to think that a more direct admission of his anger, abruptness, or mistake in extending several sessions beyond the allotted time would satisfy the patient and more readily allow her to get back to work would be a mistake and counterproductive. The therapist's steady focus on the patient's active role in her unhappiness, although often difficult, will eventually allow her to examine this aspect of her problems objectively, provided the therapist can himself remain objective and neutral in his responses to the patient's transference provocations.

General Principles of
———— Countertransference Interpretations ————

These examples illustrate countertransference in response to sadomasochistic provocation. Many other issues are likely to stir up countertransference responses in therapists. Although it would be impossible to describe and discuss even a small fraction of the possibilities, the general principles of interpretation around countertransference issues can be outlined. The first has already been discussed earlier in the chapter. Countertransference can provide important information for interpretation about the patient, in that many countertransference difficulties are induced or provoked by the patient. These provocations are sometimes obvious; at other times, they are more hidden and unconsciously determined. On occasion, they are only recognized by the therapist in his careful scrutiny of his unwitting response to them. Countertransference responses initially interfere with the therapist's understanding and proper management of the treatment. Careful thought may allow him to understand both the reasons for his untherapeutic responses and those characteristics of the patient that play a role in inducing such responses. This self-analysis should permit the therapist to reestablish his usual neutral therapeutic role and may help clarify interpretations of previously hidden material about the patient.

The next principle of countertransference interpretation has been presented in conjunction with the clinical examples. What should be interpreted is information the countertransference reveals about the patient, not what it reveals about the therapist. At times, an indirect acknowledgment of an error may be included in an interpretation, as in the second example, but this should neither be confessional nor elaborate and should only follow countertransference responses the patient is clearly aware of. The emphasis of such interpretations should be on the patient, either on his role in stirring up the countertransference or on his responses to it. The therapist should hold fast to such a position, even in the face of considerable pressure from the patient to dwell on the therapist's contributions to the problem. Such pressure comes from several sources. Probably the most important is the impact on the patient of an awareness of areas of conflict in the therapist. It is imperative that the therapist be able to manage such temporary eruptions of conflict within himself in response to the patient without making them the focus of treatment or the patient's problem via unnecessary self-revelation. Besides the unconscious wish for possible further transference gratification that may be behind the patient's pressuring the therapist following a countertransference error, the patient needs to reassure himself that the therapist has managed his difficulty and regained his neutrality and objectivity. This is essential if the patient is to feel safe in again allowing his inner feelings and wishes to be directed toward the therapist, particularly in their more insistent, regressive form. Such pressure should be considered a test by the patient to reassure himself that the therapist has regained internal order and that it is safe to proceed. Guilty confessions, self-revelations, transient gratifications, and other departures from the therapist's usual activity signal the therapist's continuing difficulties and interfere with any further progress.

Another principle of countertransference interpretation concerns the decision about whether to interpret. The occurrence of countertransference does not automatically signal the need to make an interpretation. This decision should be based upon whether the material revealed is in keeping with the main current themes in the therapeutic work, whether such material is new, particularly illustrative, emotionally compelling, or useful in elaborating or working through previously uncovered material. Care should be taken not to interpret merely out of guilt or discomfort over countertransference feelings. In general, countertransference interpretations should be rare, in the same way countertransference problems should occur only occasionally in work with a particular patient. When such problems, and interpretations based upon them, become too regular and central a part of the treatment, the therapist must explore his difficulties more intensely and may need to consult a colleague or supervisor in order to understand and resolve the countertransference. On occasion, it may even be necessary to refer the patient to another therapist, although such a circumstance ought to be carefully thought through. Such difficulties usually signal deep-seated problems that would interfere with all the therapist's work, rather than just with the patient with whom these problems seem most obvious.

The last principle of countertransference-based interpretations concerns making them as useful as possible to the patient. The countertransference difficulties that most often lead to useful interpretations are related to unconscious transference provocations by the patient. These countertransference reactions often reveal to the therapist important information about unconscious forces in the patient. Countertransference problems that are not, in this sense, reciprocal to the patient's transference distortions and provocations usually concern aspects of personal conflict in the therapist that need not be brought into the treatment via interpretations. Thus, to put it differently, most countertransference-based interpretations are a special form of transference interpretation. The therapeutic relationship is used as a workshop for the elucidation of the patient's inner life. It is particularly important with countertransference interpretations that the patient be helped to see the relationship between the therapeutic difficulty and problems, past and present, in the patient's outside life. Even more than with more typical transference interpretations, countertransference interpretations should be linked to the rest of the patient's difficulties. This is because the therapist's countertransference responses to the patient's transference distortions and pressures gives the transference a reality and measure of gratification that interferes with the patient's ability to observe objectively how such distortions are merely another version of a long-standing interpersonal difficulty. They often seem to the patient particularly situation-specific and bound up with the therapist's temporary failure to remain neutral. The patient's anxiety over the therapist's vulnerability and the need for reassurance over the safety of the therapeutic setting, usually provided by the therapist's objectivity and neutrality, further interfere with the patient's capacity to generalize from countertransference interpretations. Therefore, the therapist should take particular care to link, when possible, transference-countertransference distortions to the patient's longstanding difficulties. Thus, in the second clinical vignette in this chapter, the therapist might draw a parallel between the patient's arranging to be interrupted and turned away by the therapist and other instances in which the patient appears to give someone no choice but to hurt her. This may occur as part of the interpretation or by referring back to the incident in later interpretations. Such links should be spelled out in some detail to help patients use insights gained in a highly emotional situation in which their capacity for self-observation and reflection is limited. Especially in such instances, referring back to countertransference interpretations, and to the events that surround them, made at a time when the patient is less emotionally stirred up, is a particularly important part of the working-through process that maximizes the usefulness of the entire interpretive process.

_____ Suggested Readings _____

Kernberg, O. (1965). Notes on countertransference. *Journal of the American Psychoanalytic Association* 13:38–56.
> This paper describes two general groups of meanings of counter-transference, a narrow "classical" group referring to neurotic difficulties in the therapist that interfere with treatment and a "totalistic" group, encompassing the total emotional reaction of the therapist to the patient. The author describes the potential uses of countertransference, particularly in relation to severe regressions in patients. The clinical manifestations of certain chronic countertransference problems are described and the "concern" for the patient in the therapist as a source of protection against these problems is discussed. Realistic limitations, preconditions, and characteristics of therapeutic concern are described.

Langs, R. (1975a). The patient's unconscious perception of the therapist's errors. In *Tactics and Techniques in Psychoanalytic Therapy.* Vol. II. *Countertransference.* Ed. P. Giovacchini. pp. 239–250. New York: Jason Aronson.
> This paper addresses the patient's sensitivity to unconscious processes in the therapist that lead to errors in technique. It is pertinent to a discussion of the handling of countertransference problems and the issue of countertransference interpretation and provides useful clinical illustrations, a characteristic of all the author's written contributions.

Langs, R. (1975c). Therapeutic misalliances. *International Journal of Psychoanalytic Psychotherapy* 4:77–105.
> This work describes nontherapeutic collusions that take place between therapist and patient, which are unconsciously designed to distort, disguise, or avoid the emergence of certain issues in the therapy. They are based upon countertransference problems in the therapist that seriously compromise the success of the treatment unless recognized and resolved.

Reich, A. (1960). Further remarks on countertransference. *International Journal of Psycho-Analysis* 41:389–395.
> In this paper, the author notes the growing divergence in the meanings of the term countertransference as it is used by different psychoanalytic schools. She compares and contrasts these meanings and applications of the concept and is, in general, critical of the Kleinian school, which uses the term to encompass all the therapist's emotional responses to the patient. The paper is

worthwhile as a statement of the most traditional psychoanalytic view of countertransference.

Tower, L. E. (1956). Countertransference. *Journal of the American Psychoanalytic Association* 4:224–256.

> The author describes conflicting conceptions of countertransference. She views countertransference strictly as the therapist's transference to the patient. She develops the idea that, in intense therapeutic relationships, the therapist develops a circumscribed countertransference attitude in response to the patient's transference neurosis, which can be conceptualized as a countertransference "neurosis." This can be a useful temporary phenomenon and have a catalytic effect on the progress of the treatment if correctly handled by the therapist.

Winnicott, D. W. (1949). Hate in the counter-transference. *International Journal of Psycho-Analysis* 30:69–74.

> This often-cited paper describes, in the author's usual imaginative and somewhat idiosyncratic way, countertransference in its broadest sense, outlining the therapist's negative reactions to the patient and how they can become interferences if not acknowledged by the therapist, both to himself and to the patient in interpretations. The author is speaking primarily of work with psychotic patients, in which the patient's and the therapist's aggression, because of its frightening, primitive, and pervasive nature, is often avoided or disguised by what the author describes as defensive sentimentality. This frequently takes the form of interpretive and interactive focus on supportive, accepting, loving feelings that deny what are usually the patient's most immediate and genuine feelings. This reference is included as an example of countertransference as used to describe the therapist's total emotional response to the patient and to illustrate a view of interpreting countertransference typical of a certain group of British analysts influenced by the work of Melanie Klein.

7

Special Problems
and Their Interpretation

This chapter covers problems met with in the treatment of certain kinds of difficult patients and other situations in treatment that require special handling. These situations raise interpretive issues about which students most often ask questions. It is important to realize that, despite the different ways in which these varied problems interfere with many different aspects of the process of therapy and in fact may threaten to break off treatment entirely, they are all best dealt with by appropriate interpretive interventions rather than by any major alteration in technique or in the therapeutic situation and its boundaries.

Acting Out

Acting out is a term whose meaning has gradually grown more diffuse and, thus, less useful over time. Acting out originally referred to those instances in which the patient involves himself in some activity in order to keep certain material out of the therapeutic dialogue. An important motive for the activity is to avoid therapeutic exploration of some hidden feeling, wish, fantasy, or memory to which the activity is related. For example, a male patient might unexpectedly become involved in an intense sexual relationship with a friend's wife right at a time when sexual feelings toward his female therapist threaten to emerge. The patient can be said to be acting out forbidden sexual wishes in order to avoid their exploration in the treatment. This substitution of activity for reflection and therapeutic exploration, which is central to acting out, is also the reason why meaning and usage of the term has expanded. Acting out has come to mean any "misbehaving" by patients. Adolescent patients, for whom delay and reflection are particularly difficult, are always described in mental health settings as acting out, when what is actually being referred to is their activity proneness, low frustration tolerance, and tendency to challenge externally imposed limits by rebellious, rule-testing behavior. In this section, the term acting out will be used in its original, limited, and most therapeutically relevant meaning.

Acting out should be understood and interpreted as a particular form of resistance in which the behavior functions both as a means of avoiding the direct introduction of certain material into the treatment as well as an indirect means of communicating the presence of such material. Acting out should be taken to signify the near readiness of the material to enter consciousness in an undisguised form. It goes beyond mere repression. In this regard, acting out is like a slip of the tongue, which also forces certain material into the field of scrutiny yet contains some measure of avoidance of recognition or acceptance of the material's full meaning. Like the slip, acting out, when recognized, should always be interpreted. This is particularly important because the unconscious pressure to act out may lead the patient to undertake dangerous actions, not easily reversible, or in other ways injurious. Such actions should be considered by-products of the treatment and any lasting negative effects viewed as iatrogenic. Thus, the therapist's attitude toward acting out may appear somewhat different from his neutral, nonjudgmental response to other behaviors or activities the patient involves himself in, although in such instances, there may also be times when the therapist should intervene to protect the patient. Acting out must be recognized in its communicative aspect. It is a way the patient tells things to the therapist in actions. If the therapist fails to "hear" these communications, acting out usually escalates, sometimes in ways that seriously endanger the patient's welfare. Some theorists speak of acting out within the transference. They are referring to certain transference manifestations as a form of acting out certain wishes and fantasies with the therapist instead of remembering them in relation to parental figures. Here, too, failure to interpret transference material often leads to an escalation in acting out, and ultimately, interference in the therapeutic process, although I feel this way of talking about "acting out" within the treatment setting further dilutes the term's meaning.

Having established that acting out should always be interpreted, that it is, in a sense, the therapist's responsibility to do so in a timely way, how should the interpretations be made? The interpretations should connect the activity and the material being kept out of the therapy. They should take into account why the patient feels threatened or otherwise reluctant to bring the material into the treatment more directly. Care should be taken not to take on a critical or directive attitude in the sense of "demanding" that the patient refrain from acting out. Acting out regularly stops when it is adequately interpreted, although it may reappear at a later time in the treatment.

> During the second year of treatment, a depressed patient was working on his problems with authority figures, toward whom he usually behaved in a consciously respectful, but covertly resentful, fearful manner. In the transference, there was considerable idealization of the therapist. The patient

seemed to be profiting from the therapy, with some clear changes in his relationship to his superiors at work. The patient consciously connected these changes to the therapist's interpretations about his competitive, frightening wishes and feelings toward his father.

In the middle of this phase of the treatment, the patient reported he was planning to buy a larger home. The therapist was perplexed, because the patient seemed to have little need of a larger home, spoke regularly of financial difficulties, and most importantly, seemed somewhat driven to make this purchase. This last feature made the therapist most suspicious that something was being hidden in the wish to buy an expensive, expansive home. As the therapist listened more closely, he observed that the patient would begin to ruminate about the purchase following any interpretation made by the therapist. The patient remarked at one point that the therapist's comments about his authority struggles were right on the money. His next association was about where he would find the money to buy the "magnificent" house he had seen the previous week, a house he felt he absolutely had to have.

Therapist: I think the pressure you feel to buy this house is a response to my "right on the money" interpretations.
Patient: What do you mean? What pressure? You know, I resent your saying that. I'm a big boy. You've never told me what to do before.
Therapist: I think my "right on the money" comments, despite helping you to see certain things more clearly, make you feel belittled and that buying a big house is to help you not feel like a little boy in relation to me.

The patient said little else during the session. When he returned, he reported angrily vowing to himself to buy this house, no matter how much it cost. The intensity of his anger in response to the interpretation led him to realize that perhaps the therapist was on to something. There followed an exploration of the patient's feelings about the therapist knowing him so well. The patient admitted he did feel belittled and resentful about the therapist's interventions,

which seemed to him "smugly knowing." Yet he also be-
lieved this response in himself was unwarranted. He often
told himself that he ought to be grateful rather than resentful because what he was learning about himself was helpful.
Thus, he kept quiet about these feelings. As therapeutic
work continued, feeling belittled, feeling like a little boy,
and wanting something big and magnificent, in all its ramifi-
cations, remained central themes. The patient's pressure to
purchase a house abated. A year or so later in the treatment,
a similar sequence around buying a car occurred; this time
without requiring any interpretation from the therapist, the
patient recognized the pressured feeling as an indication
that his conscious need to buy a car was being fueled by
unconscious processes worth uncovering in order to avoid a
potentially costly mistake.

This vignette illustrates typical acting out in its narrow
definition. Purchasing a large, expensive house, or at least
feeling pressured and preoccupied with thoughts about buying one, served to keep the patient's feelings of being belittled by the therapist out of awareness and outside the
therapeutic dialogue. Alerted by the pressured quality of the
patient's ruminating about this purchase and the temporal
sequence and content of the patient's associations regarding
this purchase following interpretations, the therapist realized
that the patient was acting out. He called the patient's attention to the connection between his response to interpretations and his pressure to buy the house. The therapist did
not tell the patient what to do. Rather, he explained in his
interpretation what he understood as the reason for the
patient's actions in terms of material being avoided in the
treatment. Interpretations of acting out should seek to avoid
specifically advising the patient about what to do or not do.
Although many patients, including the one in this example,
respond to interpretations of acting out as a departure from
the therapist's usual neutral position regarding extratherapeutic activity, the therapist, in fact, offers only an explanatory interpretation. Yet there is, in such interpretations, an
implicit message to reconsider, to reflect, to examine prior to

acting. This is important in any analytic approach, and the therapist therefore need not feel defensive about this aspect of his interpretive work on acting out. Because of the powerful forces therapy stirs up, the therapist is responsible for actively interpreting acting out to protect the patient from harm. The patient's resentful feelings about being told what to do, feeling criticized, feeling thwarted in some activity or planned activity often are related in some way to the material being avoided and should be actively interpreted. Thus, in this example, feeling resentful and being a "big boy" were very much related to the material being acted out.

In summary, acting out is another of the many different ways patients reveal otherwise hidden material about their inner lives, in this instance, about material specifically being kept out of the therapeutic dialogue by the activity itself. Acting out should be interpreted in a manner that links the activity to the treatment situation and explains the acting out in terms of specific feelings, thoughts, memories, and fantasies that are being warded off. When acting out comes to the therapist's attention, it should be interpreted rather than allowed to continue without comment. Acting out occurs in most extended treatments and should always be considered as a possible explanation of otherwise surprising or unexpected behavior.

 Character Resistances

The interpretation of resistances that are embedded in the patient's character structure presents a difficult problem for the therapist and patient to overcome. Character is a summary term for a person's typical ways of resolving tensions among conflicting mental trends. It is determined especially by the various identifications that shape the configuration of the psychic structures involved in the patient's internal struggles. Identifications with various aspects of the parental objects are the major determinants of character. These identifications are deeply embedded and give to character what is described as its permanent and automatic quality. Although a complete exposition of the treatment of character problems is beyond the scope of this discussion, certain principles of interpretation of character resistances will be described. In many ways, these principles lie at the heart of a more general treatment approach aimed at character change.

Patients do not view their character problems in the same way they view their symptoms or their interpersonal difficulties. Although they are often aware, in a general way, of aspects of their character structure that interfere with their happiness or productivity, patients experience their character traits as automatic, permanent, or, in technical jargon, ego-syntonic. To patients, character is who they are and how they always feel and act. Most of the processes that shape what is called character are unconscious and go unnoticed by the patient. Often other people complain about or suffer from the patient's character problems.

Character resistances appear in therapy when the interpretive work leads in a direction of change that is "out of character" for the patient. We call it a character resistance when the patient seems not to be fighting the change by any specific activity. Rather, there is the sense that the change is something the patient never does. For example, an obsessional patient, having worked out a specific conflict with an authority figure that had led to much passive-aggressive behavior, is observed to continue to approach this person in the same guilty, resentful, and subtly provocative way he has always dealt with him and others in similar positions. Another kind of character resistance occurs when an aspect of the patient's character interferes with his cooperative efforts in the treatment. For example, an obsessional patient, who must always be in control, is unable to free associate for fear that irrational, "dirty contents" will spill out. Or a masochistic patient experiences all the therapist's interpretations as painful wounding attacks and thus loses sight of their useful content. These are not situation-specific phenomena, but rather occur in all the patient's interactions. For the most part, the patient is unaware of them.

The first phase of the interpretive process with regard to character problems is to make the patient aware of that aspect of their character that is interfering. The goal here is to make something that has been automatic and natural feeling to the patient stand out from the rest of his behavior. It must lose its automatic nature and become the subject of observation and reflection. This is not an easy task and should be approached carefully. Most patients respond to confrontative interpretations of character resistances only after they are made repeatedly, but without impatience or criticism. Since patients view character as part of, or integral to, themselves, to their way of seeing themselves, they easily feel personally attacked by character interpretations. That is why it becomes so important to attempt to isolate the particular resistant aspect of the patient's character, to make it less a part of him prior to exploring its meaning and its particular function as a resistance to the progress of the treatment. Early character interpretations should merely call the patient's attention to what he is doing, with some indication, either explicit or implicit, that this is but one of several things he might choose to do. This issue of choosing, of options, of other possibilities, of the active rather than passive nature of character, is of great importance. In this regard, the therapist should also note, whenever the patient does something that is "out of character," that it is different from what the patient usually does. This can help the patient to see that he is not "just that way," but rather is "other ways too," at least under certain circumstances. A comment from the therapist, such as "so you are also tender and emotional," can help an overly controlled and severe patient recognize that he is making choices in being controlled and severe. Similarly, when the therapist notes the patient's typical response, he should do so using the active rather than the passive voice. The therapist might note "how often we see that you don't finish your work or delay doing so as long as possible in response to instructions," in commenting on what the patient might describe as "being unable to please my boss because I can't concentrate."

When the character resistance has been isolated from the rest of the patient's behavior and recognized by the patient as interfering with the treatment's progress, and usually with many other areas of his life as well, the therapist can begin to explore and interpret its unconscious meanings and its roots in the past. Most often, the behavior will be recognizable as similar to a prominent aspect of one of the patient's parents. It is not unusual that it will represent precisely that attribute of the parent that the patient has had most difficulty with in the past and has complained about, not fully recognizing to what degree it has become a part of his own character structure. At other times, the parental identification may be less obvious or absent. The interpretation of an identification should not give the impression that it is not really the patient who is actively behaving in a particular way. Rather, the trait should be understood from two perspectives. First, how does the particular character trait enter into the patient's conflicts or represent certain typical resolutions or compromises? Put differently, what are the various conflictual determinants of the behavior in question? For example, the therapist might interpret a patient's masochistic character resistance, manifested as finding a new relationship in which to be mistreated as soon as the therapist and patient work through the current painful one, as allowing the patient to "continue to satisfy sexual and dependent wishes so long as any pleasure is masked by feelings of pain, suffering, and humiliation." Other factors, such as power and control over the object, feelings of strength and superiority in withstanding punishment, and feelings of entitlement for having suffered, may also need to be interpreted, if pertinent, to round out the patient's understanding.

The second perspective for interpretations concerns the nature of the identification, if present, upon which the trait is based. What is most important here is to understand both the reasons for the identification during childhood and the way the character trait now represents an aspect of the relationship with a parental object transformed into a structuralized conflict, which, in a sense, preserves this relationship. Thus the patient's masochistic mother may have approved of her self-defeating behavior, her sacrificing her own pleasure for that of siblings, and her loving mother for all mother had to put up with in her unhappy life. The therapist, at an appropriate time, might note "how mother seemed to reinforce your letting others take advantage of you by making you her special child, someone just like her." At a later time, the therapist might interpret "now, when you arrange to be taken advantage of, you feel mother's approval as a presence within you which keeps you from feeling alone." Or "you now often get yourself hurt whenever your self-esteem is low, in order to hang on to mother and the special child role you had with her, provided you sacrificed as she did." To these typical interpretations, it might be necessary to show the patient how the character trait is functioning as a resistance at a given time. For example, "you feel the treatment is leading you in the direction of a more open search for fun and relaxation, which threatens you with feeling alone, without mother's approving internal presence. So you have to renew your suffering in order to get her back."

As mentioned earlier, the interpretation of character resistances is very difficult and time-consuming and requires extensive working through to be effective. Patients need to be shown over and over again what they are doing and why. Most character problems require long-term, intensive psychotherapy or analysis to be significantly and permanently altered. There are many failures, even under the best of circumstances. Special care should be taken to interpret slowly, sequentially, and non-critically. It is very difficult for patients to recognize, or maintain their recognition of, their character problems. They easily feel attacked. Therapists are impatient in this sort of interpretive work and often do become critical. They frequently attempt to avoid being critical by ignoring the work of interpreting character resistances, a countertransference problem that inevitably leads to stalemates in the treatment.

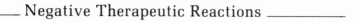

Negative Therapeutic Reactions

The negative therapeutic reaction is actually not a single entity, but rather a group of problems met with in the treatment of patients with certain kinds of character pathology. Most often, it occurs in masochistic, obsessional, and depressed patients and can be considered a specific kind of character resistance similar to those described in the previous section. A negative therapeutic reaction occurs when correct interpretive work, which would be expected to lead to some symptomatic improvement, leads instead to a worsening in the patient's condition or to some other form of failure to progress. Such situations are extremely frustrating to the therapist and are often very difficult to manage. Freud (1923) originally attributed such reactions to an unconscious sense of guilt that finds in symptoms suitable punishment so that they cannot be given up. Freud notes that such a sense of guilt can also be "taken over" from another person via identification. It is useful to think of the negative therapeutic reaction as a way in which the patient holds on to both an internal punishment or prohibition and to an object tie connected with such punishment. Thus, to improve or progress in treatment is to overcome a superego demand and to separate in some way from a powerful internal object. Until both aspects of the negative therapeutic reaction are interpreted, the stalemate will usually persist. In addition, the anger and frustration the therapist experiences in such situations often leads to countertransference difficulties that result in interpretations that subtly punish the patient further and thus aggravate the problem in the work.

When a negative therapeutic reaction occurs, the following sequence of interpretive interventions is usually in order. As with all character resistances, the patient must first be made aware of what is occurring. The patient often merely experiences the negative therapeutic reaction as a continuation of his typical painful or unsatisfying experiences. He may not recognize that anything unusual has happened. The therapist must therefore show the patient that his current response is directly related to the interpretive work that logically would be expected to lead in a direction very different from the negative response that has, in fact, occurred. Only when the patient is aware, at least descriptively, of what has happened can the interpretation of the hidden motives for the problem begin. Next, the therapist can approach the patient's need to fail or suffer, both because of guilty feelings and because this suffering was part of a tie to another person. Often the other person required such suffering as a condition for love, admiration, or attention. Frequently, they themselves were suffering, depressed, and masochistic people whose important relationships were all characterized by sadomasochistic interactions. When this object tie has been uncovered and clarified, it can usually be shown that the patient, by not improving or by getting worse, is engaging the therapist in a provocative struggle designed to hurt the therapist and to provoke his punishing responses, thus maintaining, in the transference, a relationship that perpetuates the tie to the original sadomasochistic object.

> A depressed woman with serious masochistic character pathology was working on her difficulties in losing weight. Her obesity kept her from feeling appealing around her husband, embarrassed her when she went to business meetings and met old friends and acquaintances who had known her when she was slender, and added to her low self-esteem and depressed affect. An extended period of uncovering and interpretive work led to her recognition that her guilty feeling about initiating sexual activity with her husband was historically related to her mother's attacking comments to her as a child that she ought to be ashamed of herself for allowing her father to see her naked. She could not allow herself to be flirtatious with her husband,

despite his encouragement. During one session she commented, "besides, with all this fat, I couldn't be sexy anyway." She was startled by the obviousness of her comment
in terms of revealing an important motive for her overeating. The remainder of the session was spent exploring her
childhood guilt about her seductiveness and her current
use of overeating to avoid feeling guilty about being sexy.
Her self-loathing about her obesity was explored as a
punishment, or a retaliation, for her proud exhibitionism as
a little girl. The patient seemed excited about the direction
of the work.

The next session began with the patient more depressed
and self-flagellating than ever. The patient did not mention
the work of the previous session. Her enthusiastic and
encouraged response to the interpretive exploration of her
overeating seemed to have vanished. Perplexed and disappointed, the therapist listened as the patient somewhat
monotonously recounted her familiar tale of woe.

Therapist: Yesterday's uncovering of a motive for your
overeating and the encouraged feeling you had about it
appear to have left you feeling worse than ever.
Patient: I don't see what that has to do with it.

The patient at this point continued her litany of complaints.
The therapist reiterated his conviction that there was a
connection between the correct and useful interpretive work
of the previous session and the patient's feeling worse.

Patient: How encouraged could I have been? When I left
yesterday, I went right to the supermarket and bought
cookies and stuffed myself. I felt like a defiant little kid.
Therapist: Who were you defying?
Patient: You. And my mother.

The patient noted that her mother was always critical of her
overeating, yet always kept all kinds of sweets in the house.
She recounted that, although she obeyed her mother, a controlling, intrusive, masochistic person, in almost all other
areas, she refused to deny herself food, no matter how angry
her mother got.

> *Therapist:* So, by overeating, you could, at least in one
> area, defeat her control over you, while protecting yourself
> from being accused of being sexually provocative.

The patient spoke next about how her mother dominated
her, made her guilty about any pleasure she sought, rewarded
her self-sacrifice with attention and admiration, and continued to attempt to intrude into her adult life. She cautioned
her about trusting her husband or friends, all of whom would
take advantage of her unless she remained as untrusting and
hypervigilant as her mother was.

> *Therapist:* She could not let you trust the discovery we
> seemed to make together yesterday. She required that you
> return to your suffering and thereby defeat me.

There followed a return to work on the overeating and at
least a temporary end to the negative therapeutic reaction,
although similar instances occurred throughout the treatment. In this instance, the negative therapeutic reaction was
a complicated compromise formation. It defended against
the patient's guilt about making progress in her efforts to
enjoy her sexuality. It satisfied her mother's demand that
she neither enjoy herself (her sexuality) nor trust anyone
(the analyst). It also frustrated her mother (she continued to
overeat) and the therapist (he could not help her). The therapist interpreted both the patient's guilty need to feel worse
and the object tie the feeling worse perpetuated. Most such
object ties are intensely ambivalent, as was this one. The
negative therapeutic reaction both maintained the tie (suffering, getting worse) yet also struggled against it (defiant
eating). It should be noted that the therapist knew the patient
quite well and had been treating her for some time. Negative
therapeutic reactions that can be dealt with interpretively
usually do not appear until well into the treatment. It is only
then that the therapist knows enough about the patient's
internal world to be able to understand the forces at work. It

may be that such reactions only occur in the middle and late phases in the treatment of patients with certain kinds of character pathology because it is only then that the progress in the treatment seriously threatens the integrity of the ambivalent, but powerful masochistic object tie upon which such reactions are usually based. Furthermore, it may be that the transference relationship must reach sufficient intensity that its provocative sadomasochistic nature can induce sufficient countertransference frustrations, anger, and retaliation from the therapist to satisfy one of the unconscious requirements of the patient for inducing such a reaction.

Negative therapeutic reactions are embedded in the character of the patient and occur when the character structure is threatened by progress in the treatment. Such reactions should be distinguished from negativism, general uncooperativeness, psychotic transference reactions, and other nontherapeutic developments in treatment. Negative therapeutic reactions are responses to correct interpretive work and progress in the treatment. Although not always resolvable, they should be dealt with interpretively, to show the patient how he is responding to the threatened progress of the treatment as endangering both an inner need to suffer, be punished, or deny himself, as well as interfering with an object relationship that requires his suffering, certain aspects of which are recreated in the transference. Many variations are possible, and no absolute rules of interpretation that cover all possibilities can be established. A general outline for understanding and interpreting negative therapeutic reactions has been described. The major limiting factor in the therapist's ability to deal effectively with these reactions is his countertransference response to the transference provocation inherent in most such reactions. Helplessness, passive withdrawal, usually a reaction formation against excessive anger and frustration, and interpretations that threaten, hurt, or belittle the patient are common untherapeutic responses that aggravate the situation. Patience, a thoughtful stepping-back from the patient, and especially, clarifying interpretations, which often need many repetitions, comprise the approach that works best. Often supervision or consultation with an experienced colleague is helpful.

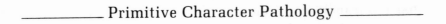

Primitive Character Pathology

Primitive character pathology refers to those patients who are usually described as having borderline and narcissistic problems. These patients are prone to repeated crises, severe regressions, suicidal behavior, and other impulse control difficulties. They often have extremely unstable, chaotic interpersonal relationships, many hypochondriacal complaints, and many other symptoms. When severely stressed, paranoid and other psychotic symptoms may appear. It is beyond the scope of this book to detail in any comprehensive manner the psychotherapeutic treatment of such patients. However, certain principles of interpretations are particularly relevant to such patients and to situations that regularly come up in their treatment.

DEFICITS AND INTERPRETATION

The most general of these principles concerns the role that the interpretive process plays in work with patients who have primitive character pathology. There are many different ways in which these patients and their pathology are described and understood. A general trend is to view such patients as having certain defects in the make-up of their psychic structures. That is to say, they cannot reconcile conflicting trends within themselves, not because of the nature of the conflicts, but rather because they do not have the equipment to do so. They therefore resort to primitive defense mechanisms involving significant distortions of reality to contain their conflicts and maintain some sense of cohesion. Denial, projection, splitting, idealizing, and devaluing are examples of such mechanisms and invade all these patients' important relationships. This leads to their interpersonal instability, unless the objects they chose have complementary psychopathology. The important or relevant point for this discussion is that these patients are conceptualized as having intrinsic ego deficits that are thought to be related to early problems in the mother–child relationship. Descriptions of the treatment of patients with such deficits all refer to the special functions that the therapist must perform for the patient until these deficits can be corrected, modified, or otherwise counteracted. Many different terms, including creating a "holding environment," "containing" the patient's pathology, and "lending" the patient ego structure, refer to the special requirements these patients have that require something from the therapist beyond what is necessary for patients with less primitive pathology.

What the therapist must do with these patients is to understand their difficulties and interpret this understanding in a manner that allows the patients to use what is interpreted profitably. This emphasis on interpretation is particularly important because much of what is written about these patients implies that, at least for a time, the therapist's main activity should be non-interpretive. This is misleading. The special requirements these patients have must be met by interpretations addressed to their special needs, not by extra kindness, not by changes in the rules and boundaries of treatment, not by "supportive" interventions in the sense of acting as advisor, teacher, parent-substitute, or any other role assumption. What is required is the steady, objective, non-judgmental, neutral therapeutic stance appropriate with all patients. The therapist "holds," "contains," "lends ego" to such patients by steadily interpreting what is going on and by not getting caught up in the intensely chaotic, transference-countertransference struggles these patients readily stir up.

Having said this much, what about the nature of the interpretations? They must be based on an understanding of the patients' particular kind of pathology. For considerable periods of time, interpretations should focus on the immediate nature of the transactions with the therapist. Such patients typically develop early, intense transference reactions without any reliable ability to observe themselves, to appraise the actual behaviors and attitudes of the therapist, or to perceive and deal with the powerful feelings stirred up in them by the treatment. The therapist must interpret within the transference far sooner than he would like, often without much information about its historical antecedents. He often must do most of the work because the patient seems perpetually caught in an emotional storm. He should focus consistently and persistently on clarifying the reality of the here-and-now interactions with the patient. These patients' tendency to project, split, and deny interferes seriously with their reality-testing functions within relationships. The therapist interprets the reality of the transactions within the therapeutic relationship. Such patients are usually powerfully attached emotionally to parental figures with whom all interactions are grossly distorted. They cannot use far-reaching explanatory or reconstructive interpretations about the development of their difficulties until the therapeutic dialogue becomes a means of a reality-oriented exchange of ideas, joint reflection, and mutual considerateness. This may take years. Usually, if it occurs at all, it will have survived innumerable crises in which the therapist's ability to understand and interpret clearly what is currently taking place has remained unshaken or at least sufficiently resilient that the focus of work remains steady. It is especially important that, in crises, the therapist make every effort to respond with interpretations rather than with judgments, advice, warnings, threats, etc. If the therapist is unable to deal interpretively with the intense affects stirred up by the patient at critical moments, then the patient will not progress in the treatment. Similarly, what the therapist interprets must be presented in a form the patient can understand and use. The therapist should delay reconstructing past traumatic experiences with parents during childhood. Although doing so in order to explain current problems in relationships is often tempting, the patient's profoundly distorted view of the parents and of childhood events, in general, make such interpretations inaccurate and ineffective. In addition, borderline patients often invite such interpretations. Providing them frequently involves joining the patient in blaming others, while obscuring the patient's active distortions of interactions in the present, especially those with the therapist. Such interpretations deflect the patient from establishing a firm reality orientation and alliance with the therapist. It cannot be overemphasized that more is required of the therapist than great patience, kindness, empathy, and resilience. He must possess these attributes, to be sure. But more importantly, he must help create for the patient a neutral, objective, reality-based language of understanding based on interpretations that accurately describe what is occurring in the therapeutic relationship.

At times, the therapist's functioning this way will be severely tested. Can he meet patients' threats of abandoning the treatment, of entering into catastrophic relationships, of committing suicide, with interpretive interventions that make such crises understandable? When are other measures really necessary? No easy answers are available. Such patients often have poor prognoses, even in the best of hands. Many die by suicide or in accidents of one kind or another in which suicidal intent cannot be accurately assessed. The therapist may be unwilling or unable to tolerate the possibly disastrous outcomes of working with such patients. In the author's experience, treatment of the kind described herein can only succeed if the therapist believes that the responsibility for the patient's safety and welfare lies primarily with the patient. If he does not feel this is the case, then he cannot respond interpretively to the events of treatment. And if he responds in some other way, the treatment usually deteriorates, the patient is in fact more endangered, and the therapeutic results will be negative.

INTERPRETING PRIMITIVE DEFENSES

As mentioned above, patients with primitive character pathology deal with emotionally difficult situations by using primitive defense mechanisms. In reality, patients do not "use" mechanisms of defense. Rather, such mechanisms are a shorthand way of describing how they make certain compromises among conflicting mental trends to protect themselves when they feel endangered. Primitive defense mechanisms are so called because they involve serious distortions of reality, because they are generally based upon developmentally early behavioral phenomena that are usually supplanted in healthier individuals by much less reality-distorting mechanisms, and because they are only poorly adaptive during adulthood. The most common primitive defenses are splitting, projection, and denial. Although it is beyond the scope of this book to explore these mechanisms in any detail, aspects of their interpretation are relevant to this discussion. First of all, because such defenses seriously distort reality, they impair all the patient's ego functions that require some measure of reality-testing. The therapist therefore must very consistently interpret the presence and meaning of these defensive reactions. In this way, the patient's reality orientation and general capacity for realistic undistorted interactions is supported.

> A woman with borderline character pathology was complaining of her unsatisfactory relationships with men. She constantly felt taken advantage of by all her partners, although there was a shameless flirtatious, suggestive quality about the patient that she neglected to comment on when she described her interactions with men.
>
> *Therapist:* Could you tell me more about what you mean by "taken advantage of"?
> *Patient:* You're like every shrink I've ever known. All you want to hear about is sex, I'm sure for your own entertainment.

The patient continued on a tirade about the therapist's morbid sexual curiosity, a tirade she seemed almost to enjoy. The therapist recognized this as a projection of her own sexual impulses. Although she was, of course, correct that the therapist was interested in her sexual life and its problems, as all therapists would be, she seriously distorted this interest as a way of disclaiming or directing attention away from her own sexual interests, which she now experienced passively as the victim of the therapist's morbid curiosity.

> *Therapist:* By directing your attention to my interest in your sexual life, you can avoid recognizing or acknowledging your own sexual impulses yet engage me in a highly charged exchange in which sex is at the center of things.

This interpretation of a projection illustrates a useful way of showing the patient the important features of a primitive defense without engaging in a battle. Because primitive defenses involve major reality distortions, they lead easily to adversarial situations in which the patient and the therapist disagree about what is real. The therapist, in this instance, interprets the shift in emphasis from the patient's to the therapist's sexual interests. He avoids insisting that the patient is wrong, since, as with many projections, there is a kernel of truth to what the patient says. The therapist also helps the patient see that her projection allows her to engage in a sexual interchange with the therapist without acknowledging her own impulses, thereby indirectly expressing and, to some extent, gratifying the impulses the defense is designed to ward off. The interpretation is made within the therapeutic relationship. It should be noted that the projection occurred when the patient felt threatened by the therapist's question about her outside relationships with men, her feelings of being taken advantage of. She immediately "sexualized" the question and distorted the therapeutic relationship. The therapist might have noted that the patient now felt taken advantage of by the therapist, just as she did by men outside of treatment. Or he might have commented on the fact that she used the words "taken advantage of," which only hinted at a sexual meaning. He then might have pointed out the way this was connected to her suggestive sexual behavior in general. Such behavior regularly led men to make sexual advances toward her, only to be perplexed by her angry rejections. Although any of these later directions of interpretation would have been accurate, the interpretation given in the example was preferable because it used the therapeutic relationship as the place to work out such reality distortions, focused on present rather than past relationships, and was clearest because the therapist could refer to his own and the patient's immediate actions to illustrate his point. Most importantly, interpretive work on other issues cannot take place with such patients when there are serious distortions in the therapeutic relationship. To a large extent, such patients experience the transference as too immediate and "real" to use as a vehicle for learning about extra-therapeutic and historically distant relationships until late in treatment.

Splitting is another defense mechanism that characterizes patients with primitive pathology. Splitting, as it is generally used, has two meanings. It refers to such patients' tendency to maintain separate internal representations of "good" and "bad" aspects of themselves and of significant objects, past and present. Such representations are not reconciled with each other, may be simultaneously conscious, and vacillate in their relative effect on these patients' moment-to-moment experience of themselves and others. Splitting also refers to the tendency of such patients to express or experience ambivalent feelings by directing the "good" feelings toward one object and the "bad" feelings toward another. This latter aspect of splitting might be thought of as the interpersonal, object-relationship manifestation of the former meaning, which refers to internalized object representations. "Good" and "bad" refer to various antithetical affective tones and their associated ideational content (i.e., love and hate, soothing and upsetting, alive and dead, close and distant, full and empty). Interpretation of splitting should focus on the simultaneous existence in the patient's experience of opposite thoughts and feelings that do not seem, in the patient's view, to be connected. Thus, the therapist might note, "when you feel I care about you less than you would like, you feel so full of hate for me you appear to lose sight of those times when my understanding of your problems leaves you feeling comfortable and contented with me to a degree you report is rare in your outside relationships." Or the therapist might note "how hard it is for you to keep clear in your thoughts her limitations at times when you are accepted by her." In commenting on the interpersonal kind of splitting, the therapist might note, "so you actively continue your search for an unconditionally kind person to love and to love you, while you totally vilify anyone who lets you down in any way." Such interpretations need to be repeated many times and illustrated over and over in the here-and-now, especially within the therapeutic relationship, for them to really be effective in counteracting splitting in primitive characters. Often one aspect of the "split" object or self-representation is projected rather than displaced. Thus the patient might himself feel loving and hated by others when in fact both are his feelings. He might feel simultaneously powerful and weak or powerful and yet belittled by others if a projection has occurred. The variations are endless and rapidly changing, requiring constant attention and interpretation to keep in focus the reality of the patient's many unintegrated feelings.

In summary, the therapist must consistently interpret such primitive defenses as splitting, denial, and projection that often occur together in various combinations. The goal is to strengthen generally the patient's reality orientation and ego functions, which are seriously impaired by these primitive mechanisms. Interpretations should focus for some time on the here-and-now and should use distortions in the therapeutic relationship as the primary illustrative data. Such work is emotionally difficult and theoretically complicated. Supervision, at all levels of expertise, is valuable and often essential. Therapeutic optimism must be tempered by realistic goals and the recognition that many such patients do poorly, despite skillful and dedicated attempts at treatment.

_____ Suggested Readings _____

Adler, G. (1979). The myth of the alliance with borderline patients. *American Journal of Psychiatry* 136:642–645.

> In this brief paper, the author questions the application of the concept of the therapeutic alliance in patients with severe character pathology. During much of the treatment of such patients, the motivating element in the therapy is a special transference development wherein the patient feels soothed, protected, and understood. It is only in later stages of the treatment that the patient is able to recognize and ally with the therapist as a real and separate person. Although the author does not spell it out in any detail in this paper, such a change in the direction of an alliance can only come with consistent interpretation of the distortions the patient introduces into the treatment relationship, along with an acceptance by the therapist of that long period of time during which no alliance as usually defined exists.

Asch, S. S. (1976). Varieties of negative therapeutic reaction and problems of technique. *Journal of the American Psychoanalytic Association* 24:383–409.

> The author reviews Freud's development of the idea of the negative therapeutic reaction. Asch views such reactions as character resistances based upon three types of ego and superego pathologies: (1) Masochistic ego distortion in response to pathology of the ego ideal; (2) "unconscious guilt," expanded to include pre-oedipal "crimes"; and (3) a special kind of character defense against severe regression to symbiotic relatedness. The author presents clinical case material illustrating these three underlying pathologies and the way they sometimes overlap. He stresses the countertransference problems such patients can induce in the therapist and advocates a steady, patient, interpretive approach.

Freud, A. (1968). Acting Out. *International Journal of Psycho-Analysis* 49:165–170.

> This brief paper describes, with the author's usual great clarity and elegance of thought, the history of acting out from its early psychoanalytic meaning of reexperiencing in the transference rather than remembering the past to its more modern usage as reenactment of the past outside of analysis. The author views

this change in meaning as resulting from a change in the analyst's interest in the direction of greater focus on ego rather than id functions, on changes in instinct theory, and on concentration on preoedipal phases that cannot be remembered within the cognitive sphere. Additionally, the treatment of sicker (non-neurotic) patients, adolescents, and children, all of whom are more prone to impulse control difficulties, has further eroded the earlier, more restricted meaning of acting out. Miss Freud takes a negative view of this diffusion in meaning. It is noteworthy that in her description of the early psychoanalytic meaning of acting out, acting out is considered a normal, expected, and desirable transference development that allows for transference interpretation of the forgotten past. Acting out in the transference is, in this context, "an indispensable addition to remembering" (p. 166).

Kernberg, O. (1976). Technical considerations in the treatment of borderline personality organization. *Journal of the American Psychoanalytic Association* 24:795–829.

This paper is a good introduction to Kernberg's views on the technical issues involved in treating patients with borderline character psychopathology. He focuses on the issue of an interpretive versus a supportive approach and emphasizes the importance of constant attention to the therapist's relative neutrality. Kernberg also describes the distinctions between psychoanalytic psychotherapy and psychoanalysis and discusses issues in going from one treatment to the other.

Modell, A. H. (1976). "The holding environment" and the therapeutic action of psychoanalysis. *Journal of the American Psychoanalytic Association* 24:285–307.

In this paper, the author describes phases in the treatment of patients with narcissistic character disorders. He delineates the therapist's holding function, a metaphoric way of describing the sense of security and protection the therapeutic environment provides. Modell examines the interpretive process in relation to the holding environment, both in establishing and maintaining it, and in leading to the dissolution of magical fantasies associated with it.

Moore, B. E. (1968). Contribution to symposium on acting out. *International Journal of Psycho-Analysis* 49:182–184.

This paper characterizes acting out as the projection of self and object representations that are part of transference fantasies, stimulated by a current situation, but reflecting earlier, repressed psychic events, in a concretistic reenactment of unconscious mental content outside the treatment setting. Moore traces this tendency to difficulties in the separation-individuation phase of development, a period during which motor activity rather than speech and thought is the primary means both of separating, and, if traumatized, "of preserving either the object or the self by escape to more displaced objects" (p. 184).

Olinick, S. L. (1964). The negative therapeutic reaction. *International Journal of Psycho-Analysis* 45:540–548.

Olinick describes the negative therapeutic reaction in response to accurate and appropriate interpretive efforts as a special kind of negativism in a sadomasochistic person prone to depression. It is a category of superego resistance directed against expected inner loss and helpless regression to a primary identification with a depressed and often similarly sadomasochistic mother. The author describes the technical management of these reactions, which usually occur when the latent positive transference with its forbidden positive feelings presses for expression.

Rangell, L. (1968). A point of view on acting out. *International Journal of Psycho-Analysis* 49:195–201.

This paper reviews the history of acting out within psychoanalysis proper and arrives at a narrow definition consonant with the one presented in this book. Acting out has, as one of its purposes, to keep material out of the therapeutic dialogue. Rangell examines the relationship of acting out to action or activity, in general, and comments on the appropriate therapeutic attitude toward each.

Reich, W. (1949). *Character Analysis*. New York: Noonday Press.

This work is of great historical importance in its emphasis on the need for sustained efforts at interpreting character resistances. Although one can disregard Reich's later formulations that occupy the last third of this work, his clear and detailed descriptions of the interpretation of character resistances are worth careful study for what they reveal both theoretically and technically about the interpretation of resistance and about the nature of character pathology.

Schafer, R. (1982). Problems of technique in character analysis. *Bulletin of the Association for Psychoanalytic Medicine* 21: 91–99.

This paper focuses on some of the difficulties in working on character resistances in treatment. Schafer outlines common interpretive problems. He particularly underscores the importance of interpreting flux and contradiction in the identifications uncovered, especially as they are revealed in surprising or uncharacteristic behaviors or feelings in the patient. Emphasis is placed on avoiding a sense of forcing the issue of change, thereby creating an adversarial rather than a neutral interpretive stance.

8

Termination Interpretations

During the termination phase of therapy, interpretations are lent a particular urgency by the anticipation of separation from both the therapeutic process, at least in its formal aspects, and from the therapist, who has become a uniquely important person in the patient's life. In discussing termination phase interpretations, those issues that can be expected to emerge with most patients, regardless of their particular personal difficulties or diagnostic category, will be emphasized. Put another way, the focus will be on the conflicts, wishes, and fantasies and their derivatives that are inherent in or regularly activated by the termination process. It must be mentioned at the outset that there are very important differences between terminating therapy that has been allowed to continue until both participants decide together that the work is at an end and those treatments that terminate for financial, administrative, or other reasons. Similarly, terminating a six-month weekly psychotherapy is vastly different from ending a seven-year analysis. Nevertheless, certain common termination issues can be identified, which will be discussed here with a view toward defining principles of interpretation generally relevant to this phase of the treatment process.

_____ The Interpretive Posture at Termination _____

To begin with, it is important to note that no radical shift in the mode or manner of the interpretive process should be instituted by the therapist as termination approaches. It is true that in more extended psychotherapies and in analysis the patient is often able to take an ever larger role in the interpretation process toward the end of the work. However, this is a natural outgrowth of the patient's increased familiarity with his unconscious processes, rather than any abrupt or strategically designed move on the therapist's part to encourage or otherwise foster the termination process by playing a less visible role. The issues of termination should be approached from the same interpretive posture as previously explored material. For that matter, there is no reason to alter significantly any other major aspect of the therapist's relationship with the patient. This brings up the issue of resolution of the transference, already discussed in Chapter 5. The patient's transference can be expected to continue, although in attenuated form, through termination and even beyond. At times, some investigators suggest, certain transference attitudes and more general regressive and dependent trends in the therapeutic relationship seem difficult to resolve or reverse in the usual interpretive way and require a change in the therapeutic posture of the therapist. Patients seem to be "stuck," and the "stickiness" poses problems for the termination work. Freud (1937), at least in part, viewed this phenomenon in relation to termination as reflecting constitutional variations in the intensity of certain drive elements that make it difficult for the patient to modify certain behaviors even after adequate interpretation. Suggested changes in the therapeutic posture are aimed at reducing or

revising the regressive "tilt" of the treatment setting by
emphasizing the "real," here-and-now, adult-to-adult relationship between the therapist and patient. Some suggest a
certain "relaxation" in the therapist's abstinent, neutral, and
anonymous posture in order to encourage a giving up or
resolution of transference atittudes toward the therapist.
Such changes in the therapist's posture or attitude are, in
the long run, counterproductive, unnecessary, and to be
avoided for several reasons. First, they may imply to the patient that the therapist's previously steady, reliable, and if
correctly managed, not too unnatural attitude, was in fact
manufactured or contrived. This will seriously interfere
with the patient's convictions about the understanding he
has gained from exploring his transference reactions to the
therapist. He may feel maneuvered into having had these
reactions if the therapist suddenly changes his behavior.
Second, a "friendlier," more open attitude may hold out to
the patient some hope for a "friendship" with the therapist
after termination, which is unrealistic. This seriously interferes with working through the loss of the therapist in the
termination work, and especially negative attitudes that get
lost in the newfound "warmth" of the relationship. Last,
since such changes supposedly emphasize the reality relationship between patient and therapist, they imply that
transference elements must or should be totally resolved at
termination, that the therapist must become "just another
person" to the patient. Many transference attitudes last well
beyond termination and require some distance from the
therapist for the patient to work through them. The therapist may remain a "special" person with whom the patient
continues to carry on a silent self-analytic dialogue long
after termination. This might be thought of as analogous to
the special position parents have in everyone's psychic life,
such that they continue to evoke certain regressive trends in
their children. Parents are never totally relieved of the
distortions brought about by the long period of dependence
upon them during childhood. What determines whether this
is pathological is a matter of degree. The same is true of the
remnants of the transference at termination and beyond. The

therapist need not and should not alter his behaviors, attitudes, and modes of interacting with the patient as termination approaches. His interpretive posture should be one of
maximizing the patient's understanding of his difficulties as
they are experienced under the stress of the impending
separation.

_____ Interpreting Termination Issues _____

The patient's response to the termination should be understood in terms of the important conflicts identified during
the previous work as they are played out around leaving the
therapist. This is, of course, a general phenomenon. Many
highly specific and idiosyncratic meanings of separation for
certain patients may be somewhat removed or separate from
the central conflicts worked on in the treatment. For example, the separation from the therapist may bring to the fore
previously hidden memories, fantasies, and other important
material about a person, lost to the patient during childhood,
who had not seemed very important during earlier therapeutic work. Or a temporary separation from the parents
during childhood may take on new, more compelling meanings. New issues may emerge, or the patient may renew his
efforts to work on certain problems "before it is too late."
Yet in a general way, the therapist can expect the central
material of the therapeutic work to color the patient's experience of ending the treatment in a way that allows for
further interpretation and working through of central themes
around core conflicts, examples of which will be presented
below. It should be noted here that there will be great differences in this regard between brief and long-term therapies. In the former, little real conflict resolution can be
expected to have taken place. Thus conflicts will emerge in
full force, whereas in terminations of long-term treatments,
previously explored conflicts may be revitalized by the stress
of termination, but often in attenuated form. There will be a
backlog of interpretive work that allows for more ready

interpretation and working through than is possible in brief treatments. It might be added here that, in brief treatments, the reappearance in full force of previously worked on, but only partially worked through conflicts at the time of termination may lead to an unnecessarily pessimistic evaluation, by patient and therapist alike, of the value of the limited work done together. Many patients, even in the face of appearing at their worst at termination, are able to benefit from the interpretive work that has been done in time-limited treatment in situations less stressful than termination. Furthermore, patients are often unconsciously motivated to appear sickest at termination to "hold on" to the therapist, to somehow avoid losing the therapist, a dynamic phenomenon that, when present, should always be interpreted.

Separation from the therapist at termination provides an opportunity for interpretive work on the ambivalence that is part of all significant object relationships throughout life. Regardless of the kind of difficulties the patient brings to treatment or the level of severity of impairment, the patient's conflicts with the key figures in his life will reflect one or another form of this ambivalence, as will the transference relationship with the therapist. The obsessional patient will manifest a cooperative, obedient, submissive attitude toward the therapist as well as a rebellious, withholding, resentful, hateful attitude, with variations as to which consciously predominates at any one time. Similarly, hysterical patients will, at times, be open, warm, seductive, and hard-working, only to become closed, cold, guilty, and resistant when other aspects of their conflicted inner lives are in ascendancy. The borderline patient may constantly vacillate between unquestioning positive regard and total devaluation, hatred, and distance. The narcissistic patient will idealize and devalue both the therapist and himself, and will be cooperative, pleasant, and involved, as well as obstructionistic, enraged, and remote, depending upon the narcissistic equilibrium in the transference at a given time. These admittedly over-simplified descriptions of conflictual patterns of interaction typically seen in various kinds of personality configurations illustrate the forms of ambivalence that will appear as the patient fashions a relationship with the therapist. In successful therapeutic work, the patient will become familiar with these conflicting attitudes through the therapist's interpretations. They will be highlighted and clarified by the therapist's neutral responses to the provocations these attitudes or strivings bring to bear on the therapeutic relationship. As termination and ultimate separation from the therapist approach, these ambivalent attitudes or conflicts will become particularly intense. In giving up an important object, the patient must work through both the positive and negative aspects of the object tie. Here an important interpretive stance with regard to termination becomes apparent. The therapist must be particularly attentive to both sides of the patient's ambivalent attitudes about him. In a general way, the therapist should assess the prevailing conscious tone of the patient's associations about termination against the backdrop of his understanding of the central conflicts worked on in the treatment. He should attempt to discern and interpret those hidden feelings, wishes, and fantasies that reflect the other polarity of these central conflicts.

A 28-year-old graduate student was seen in weekly psychotherapy in a university mental health clinic that provided one year of individual psychotherapy for students and faculty as part of a prepaid health plan. The patient had sought treatment for problems related to obsessional character difficulties. During the treatment, the main body of interpretive work centered on his need to control his feelings, his avoidance of intimacy and pleasurable experiences, particularly sexual ones, which to him meant losing control and feeling vulnerable and childish, and his persistently overcompliant, fearfully deferential, and ingratiating attitude toward anyone he saw as an authority figure. Much work was done on uncovering the obvious underlying resentfulness and passive-aggressive spitefulness that interfered with most of his relationships, despite his efforts to be pleasant and cooperative. Most of his peers viewed him as a quietly angry, sarcastic person and they tended to avoid him, except in superficial encounters. During the treatment, the patient became more able to express anger and resentment openly and thus was less prone to brooding about feeling hurt and mistreated. His social relationships improved somewhat, as did his interactions with authority figures, particularly after exploration of his resentful, competitive, yet fearful relationship with his father, which was, to some extent, reenacted in the transference.

The termination of the treatment was determined by the administrative arrangement of the university health service, which provided for one year of treatment. The therapist and patient both felt their work together had been valuable to the patient, but that much had been left undone. The patient tentatively planned to continue his therapy after graduation when and if time and financial considerations allowed. As termination approached, the patient's associations centered on his resentful feelings about having to stop. Much of his anger was directed at "the administration," the university, and the arbitrariness of the termination date. The therapist recognized this as a displacement of feelings away from him to impersonal objects, the university, the administration, and the "rules."

Therapist: I think you are angry at me for not finding a way to avoid having to say goodbye to each other, but you are reluctant to express this to me directly.

This interpretation illustrates several key interpretive principles that regularly apply at termination, although they are certainly not limited to the end of treatment. The therapist interprets the patient's difficulty in directly expressing negative feelings by noting the displacement away from him of angry feelings. This had been a central theme of the therapeutic work and thus could be expected to color the patient's way of dealing with termination, offering new opportunities for exploration and interpretation of the patient's conflicts about aggression. Another important point to note about the interpretation the therapist makes is the way the patient speaks of termination in an impersonal way, unlike the therapist, to avoid the emotional impact of separation from the therapist. Patients often speak of "the termination," the last session, ending the treatment, and so on. The therapist should be careful not to join the patient in doing this. Instead, in his interpretations regarding termination issues, he should speak of saying good-bye, of no longer seeing each other, or of parting. He should further note the patient's reluctance to speak of the termination in this way and explore why the patient chooses to avoid the full impact of separating.

In this instance, the interpretation led to the expression of considerable anger and disappointment that the therapist could not or would not do something to prevent the termination. The patient's associations centered on his fears that his anger would destroy anything beneficial that had been accomplished. He feared he would permanently alienate the therapist and felt he was being unreasonable, since he had known of the limitation on the treatment from the outset. Interpretive work on this material seemed useful and allowed the therapist to reiterate and work through earlier interpretations with the patient, particularly with regard to the patient's aggression, his fear of retaliation, and his overvaluation of reasonableness in order to control his dreaded "unreasonable" impulses. However, the therapist gradually became aware of the relative one-sidedness of the termination work. The patient, after some initial reluctance to which the therapist's interpretation was addressed, seemed "stuck" in expressing his angry, resentful, disappointed, and other negative feelings about losing his therapist. The therapist saw the patient's response in part as a logical outcome of his earlier interpretation. Furthermore, the patient had throughout the treatment been prone to respond "obediently" to leads from the therapist. He was "doing as he was told" in expressing his negative feelings directly. Yet the therapist also suspected that the patient was doing more than obeying to please the theapist, as well as attacking him with permission. He seemed to be clinging to his expressions of negative feelings. It occurred to the therapist at this point that the patient was avoiding saying anything about his affection and gratitude toward the therapist, about any feelings of sadness as the termination date approached. In a general way, he was avoiding all his positive feelings and the upcoming loss.

> *Therapist:* Our work on your anger at me could easily obscure the more tender feelings our saying good-bye stirs up in you. Have you noticed any reluctance to feel or express this other side of yourself to me?

The patient seemed taken aback by this interpretation and was silent for a moment. Painfully, he revealed that he had repeatedly fantasized about the last session and fearfully anticipated losing his composure and crying uncontrollably. Without following the course of the work beyond this point, we note the importance of helping the patient to express both positive and negative feelings about termination. Separations always stir up such ambivalent feelings, which are part of all significant relationships. The therapist should look to interpret in the direction of the missing material. This will, of course, be very different in an analysis lasting many years and in a brief weekly treatment. But in principle, both kinds of feelings about ending the relationship with the therapist must be explored.

Negative feelings are, for many patients, the most difficult ones to express during termination work. Particularly if the treatment has been valuable and relatively successful, the patient will be very much concerned with missing the therapist, with sadness about parting, and with managing without the therapist. The patient's positive feelings toward the therapist, the wish to keep him, to love and be loved by him, to express gratitude, and to hang on to the positive results of the treatment, may color the work in a way that obscures negative thoughts and affects that get lost or go unexpressed. It is particularly important that the therapist remain alert to such hidden material and help the patient realize it consciously and express it. The therapist, if he feels good about the results achieved and about the quality of the patient's relationship to him, also will experience a loss at termination, although it will be less intense than the patient's. The therapist may wish to experience the loss of the patient and of a satisfying work experience only in a positive way, which may result in a silent collusion with the patient to not explore the negative, darker side of things. This is especially unfortunate because such negative material, if left unexpressed and unexplored, will gradually undermine much of the usefulness of the work after the "positive glow" of the parting wears off. Particularly in brief treatments, in which the patient has not had much time to fully understand his problems, the insights achieved are very much tied to the person of the therapist. The unexpressed negative feelings toward him that emerge after termination can erode the patient's positive image of the therapist and thus the gains made in treatment.

Similarly, some interpretive attention should always be paid to work left undone, to conflicts either untouched or only partially resolved, to residual symptoms, to character problems, to difficulties in relationships, and the like. The results of treatment are always imperfect and limited, regardless of the patient's psychological-mindedness and enthusiasm and the therapist's skill and patience. Initially, overoptimistic expectations, whether open or hidden, must be tempered by the recognition of the power of the unconscious and of early experiences in shaping and maintaining problems, and resisting change. Accepting the limitations of treatment may be difficult for both participants in the therapy. This may play an important role in the failure to explore the dissatisfaction, disappointment, and resentment about treatment that come to the fore or are actively avoided by the patient as termination nears.

Usually the negative material can be readily discerned if the therapist remains attuned to the need to explore such ideas and feelings. Often just questioning a patient's overly positive or one-sided testimonial about some behavioral change or about the therapist or about the treatment in general is enough to begin exploration of negative material. For example, the therapist might say "you describe this change in yourself as absolute and complete in order to obscure from yourself and from me your doubts that it will last." Or "your sadness at leaving me may interfere with your recognizing certain ways in which you feel I have disappointed you or let you down." Or "you appear to feel grateful to me as well as angry and disappointed about some things left undone, yet choose to express only the positive side of your feelings for fear you will lose these good feelings or hurt me if you allow yourself to express anything negative." Other interpretations that best fit the material can be readily formulated. What is important is that the patient be helped to experience the loss of the therapist in both its positive and negative aspects, with one not being neglected to the detriment of the other.

The pressure termination places on the patient often produces a worsening of symptoms, the reappearance of previously resolved or seemingly resolved conflicts, the intensification of troublesome character traits, and other indications of regression or worsening of the patient's clinical state. Similarly, patients will often reveal new problems or previously hidden symptoms in an effort to "fix it before it's too late." Such occurrences are common, and even to be expected, and must be viewed and interpreted within the context of termination and the stress it produces. One can easily get the impression that previous therapeutic efforts were ineffective, incorrect, or grossly incomplete. Both patient and therapist are vulnerable to this tendency to devalue what has been accomplished in the face of the patient's distress and regression. This can lead to errors in interpretation. It is important that the patient's clinical deterioration be interpreted in a manner that, although taking into account the pressure of the impending separation, goes beyond merely blaming the regression on termination. Thus, interpretations such as "your phobias are coming back because you are frightened about terminating," by no means a rare kind of intervention, are far from adequate or maximally effective. Patients usually hear such interpretations as demanding they maintain their improvement rather than as clarifying or even as supportive or reassuring. The therapist should attempt to understand the clinical change in terms of the particular meaning of the termination to the patient in light of the central themes explored in the treatment.

A patient in the termination phase of a lengthy psychotherapy began to embroil herself in very upsetting power struggles with colleagues and supervisors at work long after she had apparently overcome this aspect of her chronic character difficulties. These struggles were understood both as based upon an identification with her critical, provocative mother and as a repetition of her frequent childhood fights with her mother. They occurred whenever she attempted to break with or separate herself from her mother's values, rules, and way of living. Interpretive work helped her to modify significantly her character structure, to weaken the power of this identification, and concomitantly, to give up the anxious struggling that was a way of unconsciously clinging to mother whenever she ventured into ways of behaving her mother would not have approved of.

When these struggles reappeared as termination approached, the therapist felt they were understandable in several ways. The patient was afraid that without the therapist's help she could not fight off the "power of mother within her," which was how the patient spoke of the identification. Furthermore, the loss of the therapist increased her yearning for the closeness and intimacy that, in the patient's early years, was provided only by the mother, even if in the form of controlling, sadomasochistic struggles that the patient reexperienced in her adult life by provoking fights with others. During a session in which the patient was speaking of a new problem with a colleague at work and expressing her perplexity and dismay at the return of these difficulties, the therapist made the following interpretation in response to the patient's comment that she guessed she had not really conquered this problem as thoroughly as she had thought.

> *Therapist:* Leaving me challenges whether you can ward
> off your mother's influence without me as well as leaves a
> hole that your struggles with your mother, now replaced
> with fights at work, used to fill.

Although one could argue that this interpretation should
have been divided into two different or separately made
interventions, it does represent a more far-reaching, explanatory, and integrating statement than one that merely impli-
cates termination. It emphasizes the central themes of the
earlier therapeutic work in relation to termination as a personal loss. It explains the return of old difficulties in terms
of conflicts and themes with which the patient is already
familiar. Therapists are often tempted in such instances to
overtly or indirectly accuse patients of trying to forestall
termination by unconsciously arranging to get worse. Although this, in fact, may be a motive for the clinical regression, care should be taken to help the patient understand
what is occurring rather than to assume a "weaning" position, namely, interpreting with the goal of letting the patient
know that his "ploy" will not work. It is surprising and
unfortunate how often this ends up being the case due to
poorly worded, inadequate interpretations in which the therapist really abandons a neutral, interpretive approach in
favor of one that is covertly intended to get the patient
through termination, rather than help him learn from it.

Certain subsidiary issues regarding termination interpretations are worth mentioning at this point, although they are
somewhat peripheral to the general principles of interpretation at termination. One concerns a situation that often
occurs in clinics, teaching institutions, or other settings in
which termination is followed by the patient seeking further
treatment, at times being referred by the current therapist or
at least asking for such a referral. The transfer to another
treatment and another therapist often becomes the basis of
resistance to using the termination process most constructively. Fantasies and questions about the new therapist become a way of avoiding the full impact of the loss of the
current therapist. This is especially true if the therapist

makes the referral, which is sometimes, but not necessarily always advisable. In this situation, the therapist should take care to help the patient experience and express his feelings regarding the end of their relationship. Otherwise the new therapist unconsciously becomes an extension of the present therapist, and no separation work is really possible. This often becomes the burden of the new therapist, who is left to help the patient terminate with his predecessor, a difficult, far less useful sort of termination work. Similarly, the patient may dwell on thoughts and concerns about the new treatment and attempt to enlist the therapist in joining him in anticipating the future to avoid the present. Interpreting such resistances usually requires little more than showing the patient what is occurring, along with some recognition and exploration of why saying good-bye is so difficult, painful, anxiety-provoking, or otherwise distressing. A comment such as "your concerns about what your future therapist will be like is a way of downplaying what no longer seeing me feels like to you, as understandable as these concerns about the future really are" would be an example of such an introductory interpretation. Usually such an intervention is all that is necessary, although in some patients, a more stubborn resistance is at work, which requires more extensive exploration. If a direct referral is made, it is probably always advisable to explore what this means to the patient. For example, does the patient view this as an unconditional endorsement of the future therapist, an expectation that the patient chooses to work with this therapist, or some indication that the new therapist will continue where the old one left off or will work in a similar manner?

Another issue regarding termination concerns the way in which the therapist says good-bye to the patient during the last session. As in Chapter 1, where the therapist's explanation and other opening comments to the patient are discussed, these are not, strictly speaking, interpretations, but rather interventions that can rightly be considered continuous with the interpretation process. In that chapter, it was pointed out that the patient has a right to expect something more than being ushered into a quiet room to figure out for himself what to do while the silent therapist looks on. Similarly, when the treatment is over and the time for ending the last session arrives, the patient has every reason to assume the therapist will say good-bye to him, particularly since his own feelings about the separation have been explored so carefully. To be sent off without any sort of good-bye will seem strange, uncomfortable, and unfair. Therapists, if they have been actively involved in a productive therapeutic process with the patient, will themselves experience a loss at termination and will want to say good-bye in a manner that communicates something of the two-way nature of the experience. Yet no radical departure from the therapist's stance of neutrality, relative anonymity, and strict focus on the patient's life is really desirable. This leads to a dilemma that, at times, may cause the inexperienced therapist to omit a statement of good-bye altogether. As mentioned earlier, a change in the therapist's stance, if designed, in some way, to influence the patient to give up regressive, transference attitudes in order to be able to terminate, is genuinely counterproductive and to be avoided. Saying good-bye to the patient can be managed in such a way that it is neither a manipulatively designed maneuver to emphasize the "real, here-and-now" relationship nor a radical shift in the way the therapist speaks to the patient. The therapist might simply say "I have been pleased to have been able to work with you on your problems and hope things continue to go well for you." Or "I am glad our work together has been of value to you and wish you the very best in the future." The point is not that any one statement can capture anything of the intensity of the therapeutic relationship and the feelings that ending it stir up in both participants. But the therapist should not feel constrained in saying good-bye and wishing the patient well, so long as it involves no unnecessary and confusing self-revelation (i.e., "working with you has been especially valuable to me"), avoids any obscuring of the finality of saying goodbye (i.e., "keep in touch with me"), and avoids instructions or other intrusions into the patient's future decisions (i.e., "I hope you will follow up on the plans we discussed"). A handshake or even an embrace, if the latter is initiated by the patient, reflects the power and emotion of the moment and need not be viewed negatively. The therapist must act with thoughtfulness and restraint, but not with coldness. He must recognize that his own feelings about terminating with patients can be quite powerful, but that he must work these through without the patient's help.

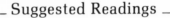

Suggested Readings

Firestein, S. K. (1974). Termination of psychoanalysis of adults: A review of the literature. *Journal of the American Psychoanalytic Association* 22:873–894.

> This review of the literature on termination makes clear the lack of consensus about termination criteria, about the technique of terminating treatment, and about the meaning of typical therapeutic events during the termination phrase. It is included here as a valuable reference in terms of literature review.

Freud, S. (1937). Analysis terminable and interminable. *Standard Edition* 23:216–253.

> Freud's only technical contribution on the termination process is this late paper that, in reality, centers less on termination than on the efficacy of the analytic method and its limitations. Freud attempts to define those factors that limit the success of treatment and offers a balanced view, judged by some as overly skeptical compared to Freud's earlier enthusiastic claims for analytic treatment, of what can and what cannot be accomplished in analysis.

Miller, I. (1965). On the return of symptoms in the terminal phase of psychoanalysis. *International Journal of Psycho-Analysis* 46:487–501.

> The author addresses the problem of a recrudescence of symptoms in response to the threat of termination and describes an interpretive approach to this common clinical phenomenon, illustrated by clinical material. He believes the reappearance of symptoms is, in fact, an indication of insufficient working through. Furthermore, it may represent an attempt to preserve certain unconscious fantasies associated with anxiety about separation.

Schafer, R. (1973b). The termination of brief psychoanalytic psychotherapy. *International Journal of Psychoanalytic Psychotherapy* 2:135–148.

> This paper describes the essential aspects of brief psychotherapy and the problems that arise at the time of termination. The author explores what can and what can't be done in brief treatment and provides a context for thinking about how the work of termination interpretation offers an opportunity to underline what has been accomplished as well as place in perspective what has been left undone.

9

General Principles of Interpretation

The interpretive process is the central therapeutic activity of the therapist. In the preceding chapters, the technique of interpretation has been described in relation to different phases of the treatment process and to various specific therapeutic issues and clinical entities. Despite the uniqueness of every patient and of every treatment, certain general principles of interpretation regarding typical instances in treatment have been described. Understanding these will help the therapist develop technical skill in interpreting and will be useful in establishing a basis for thinking about the theoretical underpinnings of interpretive technique. This final chapter will address general principles of interpretation as they apply to therapeutic technique throughout the treatment process.

_____ The Therapeutic Action of Interpretation _____

There is no consensus about which aspects of therapy are responsible for change in the patient. Furthermore, it is somewhat inaccurate to isolate one aspect of treatment from the others and discuss its role in facilitating change. Unless all the main components of the therapeutic situation are intact and functioning properly, no useful, lasting change will take place. Within psychoanalytic circles, a debate has tended to center on the relative significance of the interpretive process versus the impact of the relationship with the therapist in producing change in the patient. In non-analytic psychotherapy research, the trend has been to attempt to identify common elements in different therapeutic approaches that lead to change, it being difficult to demonstrate that one mode of treatment is clearly superior to others for a particular problem. This had led some researchers to contend that certain general or nonspecific aspects of all therapies are therapeutic and that the specific differences in technique are unimportant. Too many variables are involved to support such a contention. Yet it should be borne in mind that the question of what is therapeutic is extremely complicated and that there is much room for disagreement, debate, and further research.

The question of what is meant by the term therapeutic is itself difficult to answer. In this discussion, therapeutic refers to an increase in the patient's self-understanding and change in the patient's experience of his life in a way he and the therapist agree is beneficial. Improved relationships; greater work productivity; relief from anxiety, phobias, or other symptoms; improved self-esteem; and character changes are among the many possibilities. In focusing on what about interpretations is therapeutic, it is understood that it is the entire process of treatment that is therapeutic. Interpretations have a therapeutic action by fostering this process.

Freud (Breuer and Freud, 1895) laid the groundwork for understanding the therapeutic action of interpretations with his hypothesis that revealing to the patient repressed traumatic experiences allowed the patient to discharge troublesome emotions connected with these hidden traumas by allowing them to become conscious in the safety of the therapeutic situation. From this hypothesis grew a number of more sophisticated and complicated views of what constitutes the therapeutic action of the work of interpretation. The replacement of unconscious processes by conscious ones, where there is less distortion, is one such view. The resolution of unconscious conflicts by helping the patient to have a larger, more complete, more realistic view of the mental forces involved in such conflicts is a related concept. The reexperiencing of old conflicts, involving childhood relationships, in the present with the therapist, allowing for new outcomes of problems tied up with such relationships, is yet another way of describing the therapeutic action of treatment. There are many others. Interpretations are the main communicative means by which the therapist fosters such therapeutic actions.

Interpretations expose, clarify, question, support, contradict, remind, explain, connect. In a general way, they help the patient know more about his own mental activities. This knowledge is referred to as insight. The therapist believes that the more the patient accurately knows about himself, past and present, the better are his chances for fashioning compromises among the many conflicting forces within himself and in his environment that will improve in his life. Adaptation is a word sometimes used here. Interpretations make mental events conscious. They become objective. They are known by the patient and by the therapist. They can be examined, questioned, reevaluated. As spoken words, they have a presence, a reality with which the patient is forced to contend. The patient may have a thought. Telling this thought to the therapist gives it new meaning. Hearing the therapist say the thought adds yet another perspective. Mastery over the material is heightened. Interpretations become the patient's vocabulary for understanding new and old aspects of himself. Inherent in this view of interpretations and their therapeutic action is the idea that the patient will make the best adaptation possible for him based upon what he accurately or correctly knows about himself and his environment. Without such a view, therapy becomes directive or coercive. The working through process links the patient's new knowledge with change or new adaptation that would be expected to occur.

To summarize, interpretation is the process by which the therapist expands the patient's knowledge about himself. It is therapeutic because such expanded knowledge will lead to a beneficial change in the patient in terms of better adaptation to inner and outer needs and limitations. The therapist must feel he can count on this adaptive process. He carefully attends to any interference with it, which requires further interpretation. Many details are described throughout the book of ways in which interpretations foster the process of treatment and thus are therapeutic. Here, the general thesis of interpretation yielding insight that allows for more optimal adaptation has been described as its central therapeutic action.

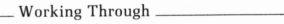

Working Through

The therapist's interpretations, to which the patient makes many contributions, become the core of the patient's new and enlarged understanding of himself. Interpretations usually refer to specific situations, past and present, but they gradually come to articulate certain themes and trends that occupy a central place in the patient's new view of his difficulties. Working through is an ongoing part of the interpretive process, wherein individual interpretations around specific instances are pieced together to form a cohesive picture of the patient's inner world. Working through involves showing the patient how something clarified by a particular interpretation fits in with the rest of his knowledge about himself. This is accomplished by demonstrating other in-

stances of similar phenomena clarified by an initial interpretation, by linking past with present, by connecting intra-
and extratherapeutic experiences, and by innumerable other
measures that add up to new and more complete understanding. Included in this process is linking insight gained
via interpretation to change in behaviors, attitudes, and
feelings. Working through thus aims at maximizing the effectiveness of the interpretive process. It occurs throughout the
treatment process, but is especially evident in later phases
of the treatment in which insight is most clearly expected to
lead to change.

Working through should be thought of as an integral part
of the interpretive process, rather than as something that
occurs after interpretations are made. Interpretations are, in
almost all cases, made in stages that reflect the current focus
of the therapeutic work. A hypothetically complete single
interpretation, which would explain a current problem in
the patient's life outside of the treatment, its counterpart
with the therapeutic relationship, its distortion in the transference, and all its significant childhood antecedents, would
be impossibly cumbersome for the therapist to make or for
the patient to comprehend. Thus it is understood that interpretations are incomplete, subject to further elaboration and
change in the light of new information. Furthermore, with
the expectation that they will lead to changes in the patient's
view of himself and in the patient's behavior, additional
work at a later time is an expected part of any interpretive
intervention aimed at behavior change. This is particularly
true given the powerful forces that, in most instances, resist
change. Patients usually need to be shown over and over
again the meaning of certain of their more pathological ways
of seeing and doing things if interpretations are to have a
lasting effect. "Working" is an apt part of the name for the
process, to the extent that it is most often difficult, repetitive, time-consuming, and frustrating, yet absolutely necessary. The image of the intuitively brilliant therapist impart-
ing pearls of insightful interpretive wisdom to the grateful,

pliable, rapidly changing patient is a myth few experienced therapists recognize as in any way related to their own experience.

Working through, as it relates to change, raises questions about the usual analytic dictum concerning the therapist's position with regard to change in the patient. Traditionally stated, the therapist helps the patient to see and understand clearly, without the distorting influence of his neurotic problems, how his difficulties have arisen and been maintained. What the patient does with this new awareness is the patient's prerogative. This dictum recognizes that, in order for the patient to feel safe to reveal himself fully to the therapist, he must feel that decisions about himself will remain his own, free of the therapist's preferences, values, and coercion. Although it is true that the ultimate choices remain the patient's, this dictum is misleading in terms of the day-to-day work of treatment. The work of interpretation invariably leads to certain directions of change the working through process is designed to foster. It is of little help to state that the therapist helps the patient to change in directions the patient chooses. Although in a general way this is correct, for long periods in the course of many therapies, the therapist exerts pressure for change against which the patient resists with all the force of the irrational at the disposal of his pathological trends. The therapist is constantly making judgments, moving the treatment and the patient in one direction or another. The working through process pushes the patient in the direction of change implied by the content of the material revealed in the interpretation being worked through. This direction of change may have little to do with those areas of life the patient initially saw as problematical and for which he sought help in changing.

> An interpretation reveals to the patient that his slowness in response to the requests of his boss is not the result of the patient's poor work skills or innate meticulousness, but rather is a deliberate, but unconscious attempt on the patient's part to thwart, frustrate, and irritate his boss. Sub-

sequent interpretations center on the patient's similar responses to other authority figures, to anyone he perceives is telling him what to do, including his wife and his friends. This behavior is traced back to his resentment of his overly controlling father, to his fearful submission to and identification with certain passive-aggressive trends in his father, which he then learned to use against him when his father wanted him to do things he resented doing. His slowness is thus understood as the continuation in the present of a childhood compromise formation based upon suppressed anger, fear of injury, and pathological identification with the aggressor.

In this typical sequence of interpretations, there is an implicit expectation that the patient will give up his slowness. One might say it is not the therapist who demands this, but rather the analysis of the unconscious meaning of the slowness. The patient does not hurry up. It becomes evident that the patient views the therapist's efforts to understand his slowness as pressure to hurry up. In the transference, the therapist-father is bullying him, ordering him to hurry up. The therapist interprets that the patient is thwarting the therapist because of feeling pressured to do something, when in fact, he very much wants to give up his slowness and has enlisted the therapist's help in accomplishing this. Yet now he is hearing, in the therapist's interpretations, his father's domineering tone. With this interpretation, the patient stops procrastinating and his work performance is noticeably better. The patient occasionally brings up instances of situations in which he formerly would have felt ordered around and would have resisted. The therapist, at times, notes how such instances do indeed resemble previously described situations that stirred up the patient's need to fight back indirectly with self-defeating slowness. Or the therapist calls attention to some specific aspect of the incident being described that most likely reactivates the patient's conflict with his father. In this way, the patient becomes ever more familiar with the details of a particular conflict, its clinical manifestations, and its childhood antecedents as they have been revealed in the interpretive work. His changed behavior is consolidated.

Where in this sequence did working through begin? Working through is a relative term with an imprecise meaning. One could argue that it began when interpretations of the meaning of the slowness did not lead to the expected change, requiring interpretation of the paternal transference, upon which the resistance to change hinged. Or one could say working through consisted of subsequent references to similar situations and to extensions of this sort of problem into other aspects of the patient's life. The interpretive process is continuous. The same material comes up over and over again throughout most treatments. At different points in the process it is viewed from different perspectives, and previous understanding is modified, amplified, and reinforced with new evidence. Working through, in a general way, means consolidating insights into the most complete understanding possible and into changes in thought, feeling, and behavior based upon this understanding.

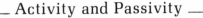

Activity and Passivity

Patients regularly experience their emotional problems as something that happens to them from without, something unwanted over which they have little or no control. One way of saying this is that the patient experiences his problems passively. A major goal of the interpretive process is to help the patient recognize that his emotional problems are, in many respects, the result of and sustained by his own mental activity. Interpretations reveal the hidden mental actions—the wishes, compromises, satisfactions, and reproaches of which the patient is largely unaware. As these actions are recognized, the patient's passive view of his problems is turned into an active one, and with this comes hope about the possibility of change. The patient becomes aware of how he repeatedly distorts his current experiences in order to recreate old, unresolved conflictual situations. He becomes conscious of motives for his hidden actions that help him to recognize why he interferes with his own success and happiness. When the patient is able to recognize and accept his own activity in maintaining his current problems, based upon the distorting influence of his past experiences, in which he also played an active role, he then is better able to consider and effect changes in himself. This will result in new compromises and solutions to conflicting trends within himself that allow for better adaptation, with more opportunities for success and satisfaction.

The entire interpretive process should be geared toward helping the patient develop a view of himself and his mental life as active, interconnected, and comprehensible. His problems should become what he does rather than what he has. The role of victim must be given up. The language of interpretation should stress the active role the patient takes. This often involves translating the patient's passive version of a situation into an active one.

> *Patient:* I found myself once again subject to one of my husband's endless and unreasonable tirades.
> *Therapist:* Although you feel a victim in such situations, we have seen how you often provoke these tirades by your husband, and then elect to suffer silently through them in order to feel mistreated in a manner similar to the way your mother felt mistreated by your father.

This interpretation emphasizes the purposefulness of experiencing something in a passive way. It specifically mentions the choice the patient makes in electing to suffer.

> *Patient:* I always end up with men who are weak, dependent, or afraid of commitments.
> *Therapist:* You feel you end up with such men by chance when, in fact, you choose them because they feel safe to you.

This interpretation again points out that what the patient wishes to see as chance is purposeful. What both these interpretations do is underline the patient's activity hidden by the apparent passivity of their conscious experience of a given situation.

The issue of responsibility is raised by most such interpretations and is, in fact, a central theme of most therapeutic work. Passivity implies blamelessness, activity requires accepting responsibility. Patients often respond to interpretations such as these by feeling the therapist is "blaming" them, when, in truth, they wish to blame others, often parents, for their problems. Interpretations that merely say "you do this to yourself," without leading toward the exploration of the motive for the patient's more passive view, do sound moralistic and blaming and are not particularly helpful. Blame and blaming are important issues in treatment and should be confronted in their own right, and their meaning to the patient should be explored. The truth is that much psychopathology does result from pathology in parents that interferes with healthy development. Chance events play a role as well, but rarely the leading one. Yet blaming one's parents has little usefulness. Neither does blaming oneself. When carefully examined, such blaming of oneself or others is in the service of avoiding making changes by continuing to portray oneself in the passive role of being permanently and negatively influenced and without choices for new behaviors that a more accurate, less distorted view of the past and present ought to allow for. As patients discover parental attitudes and behaviors that were deleterious to their development, there are very natural feelings of anger and the wish to blame. The therapist needs to intervene only when these do not give way to efforts to understand and undo these negative effects. The patient needs help in recognizing how his problems, whatever their origins, became solidified, what gratifications they allowed and continue to allow for, what form these problems took in the past and now play in current difficulties, and what measures are needed to effect change. The therapist's interpretations, even those reconstructions that describe early traumatic experiences, should underline the patient's active internalizations, distortions, and maintenance of the effects of such experiences.

Therapist: Your mother's frightening rages, and your fearful attempts to avoid her when she was agitated, you now recreate in relating to women both by acting as though you must always appease them as well as by subtly provoking their anger to see whether they will lose control as your mother did.

Such an interpretation is far preferable to one that emphasizes how the mother's rages have made the patient fearful of women. The goal should always be to help the patient see himself and his problems as his own creation, although admittedly in response to often less than ideal early experiences.

The Conflictual Context

Throughout the text, particular emphasis has been placed on interpreting within the context of the patient's conflicting wishes, prohibitions and other mental trends. There are many ways of understanding mental life besides viewing it as the outcome of conflicting forces. Certainly the patient's problems are the result of internalizations of maladaptive interactions with family members that led to the development of less than optimal psychic structures. One might speak of deficiencies in the patient's mental apparatus that interfere with adaptation. Constitutional predispositions, traumatic experiences, inadequate role models, poor parenting, and a multitude of other factors influence the way the patient meets and responds to the demands of adult relationships and experiences. Patients come to treatment with their own language and models for describing and understanding their difficulties. As outlined in the previous section, these models often, although certainly not always, are characterized by a descriptive, experiential, passive, and discontinuous view of the problems they are designed to explain. One of the goals of the interpretive process is to help the patient create for himself a less distorted, less discontinuous view of his problems and of his own activity, past and present, in creating and maintaining them. Such a dynamic view of mental life is easiest for most patients to recognize and use within the context of a conflictual framework. This does not mean that every interpretation must be slavishly constructed to highlight conflicting forces. To do so often blurs or de-emphasizes the important meaning the interpretation is designed to convey. Feelings, memories, relationships, iden-tifications, and other important aspects of mental life are not always best described, clarified, or questioned in terms of conflict. But in a general way, patients recognize that they are at war with themselves, do things, so to speak, despite themselves, and in effect, are involved in internal and inter-personal conflicts from which they are unable to extricate themselves. Interpretations should help define what these conflicts are, how they developed, and what distortions and other factors render them unresolvable in a manner that would promote the patient's best interests. Interpretations often expose and clarify those elements of the conflict the patient is least aware of or which he is most confused about or unsure of. Childhood conflict resolutions can be reworked as past distorting influences are seen as no longer pres-ent. The therapist should help the patient recognize that there are always choices to be made in resolving conflicts and that new choices are possible. The therapist's interpre-tations clarify more accurately than the patient has himself been able to do what the conflicting forces and factors in-fluencing him really are. The scene is set for new action by the patient to bring about his own recovery or to change himself. The focus is on past and present activity and the possibilities for new solutions and compromises that are more under the patient's conscious control. A conflict-centered interpretive stance discourages blaming, lamenting over de-ficiencies and past traumatic experiences, and a static or helpless view about past and present problems. Such an approach applies for neurotic and for more severe borderline, and even psychotic, problems for which theoretical views of psychopathological processes tend to emphasize deficiencies rather than intrapsychic conflict. Interpretations tied to conflictual situations are closer to the experience of all patients, no matter how disturbed, than are interventions that merely describe areas of vulnerability or shore up weakened defensive operations.

The therapist should develop a language for interpreting within a conflictual context. Often, adopting the patient's language is useful. For example, the patient may speak of being in a fight with himself about something or about wanting to overcome some constraint, reluctance, or inhibition in himself with regard to some action or feeling. In such instances, the therapist can frame his interpretations along the patient's line of expression, usually adding something about the less apparent element in the patient's fight with himself.

> *Therapist:* You both want to punish your son for having done wrong because you feel this is in his best interest, yet fear you will be too cruel, in keeping with your old worries about being unloving and nasty. Thus you get into a fight with yourself about discipline, which your son recognizes and which then leads to further provocativeness on his part.

This is a typical interpretation of a conflict. It shows the patient that he both wants to do something and wants to avoid doing the same thing because of a longstanding fear over his sadistic impulses. It expresses both conflicting trends or wishes and an explanation for the patient's inability to act satisfactorily on his seemingly more reasonable motive, his wish to punish his son. It also includes a statement about the outcome of his failure to achieve compromise. This can be made as a single or as a two-part intervention, depending on the clinical situation. By expressing both sides of the dilemma, the therapist often gets closer to what the patient feels than if he elects to interpret only one aspect of the conflict, say, the patient's fears about himself. If an interpretation captures how the patient feels, it is most likely to have more impact, to have conviction for the patient. This is perhaps the most important reason for interpreting within a conflictual framework. It also is felt by the patient to be a more neutral, less "advising" intervention than an interpretation that mentions only one side of a conflict. Had the therapist said "you are afraid to punish your son because it will cause you to feel cruel and unloving," the patient might easily have felt the therapist was pushing him to modify this aspect of his conflict. Although this would not necessarily be a poor interpretation, an interpretation that captures both sides of a conflict is technically preferable and clinically more compelling and useful to the patient.

The Timing of Interpretations

Many factors have a bearing on the decision about when to make interpretations. Some of these factors can be conceptualized as general principles of interpretation and described as technical precepts based upon accumulated clinical experience. Several such precepts will be described below. There are factors that determine when therapists make interpretations to patients that are embedded in the emotional relationship between the two participants and are largely unconscious. There are many pressures on the therapist. Most come from the patient, particularly from the patient's transference provocations that more and more come to dominate the therapeutic relationship as the treatment proceeds. At times, the therapist may have problems that have nothing to do with the patient, but that may alter his emotional equilibrium in such a way as to play a role in determining when he decides to make an interpretation. One can say that there is a balance between conscious and unconscious factors in the therapist that determines what he does.

Technical expertise enlarges the sphere of influence of the conscious, thoughtful, experience-based factors in determining when interpretations are made. This is not to say that unconscious factors are necessarily inappropriate, countertransferential, or otherwise negative in their effects. The importance of unconscious communications and perceptions between patient and therapist has been described elsewhere in the book. In the long run, conscious decision-making about interpreting, based on sound technical precepts, is far more reliable and likely to move the treatment in the desired direction than are those unconscious factors that inevitably make their presence known. This book is designed to expand the therapist's clinical expertise in the area of interpreting, in the belief that defining and clearly understanding principles of technique are the best protection against the gradual erosion of clinical skill and confidence that comes with an overreliance on empathy, intuition, and good intentions. An antitechnical bias, and the viewing of psychotherapeutic skill solely as an art or a special predilection of certain fortunately endowed individuals, is a dangerous way to approach clinical work with patients. Especially during training, when the therapist has little experience to fall back on, developing technical skills helps the therapist feel confident and avoid the sensation of merely reacting to patients. The timing of interpretations should be based, as much as possible, on thoughtful consideration based upon a sound knowledge of technical principles.

The first such principle concerns the timing of interpretations within the therapeutic hour. In general, the patient should be allowed to start the hour wherever he chooses because valuable information can be obtained from the way the patient begins. The therapist should listen to how the material unfolds during the hour and should decide what the major theme or themes are and how they relate to the previous work. If he chooses to make an interpretation, it is best if he can do so somewhere in the middle of the hour, rather than at the end, although obviously the nature of the material rather than arbitrary timing factors should be the main determinant. The advantage of making interpretations in the middle of sessions is that it gives the therapist an opportunity to hear the patient's associations following interpretations. These associations allow him to judge whether it leads to new material, to a filling in of important memories, or to a change in the patient's affective state. The patient has time to think about the interpretation with the therapist, to respond, to disagree, to elaborate. Interpretations made right at the end of the hour often feel like "parting shots" to the patient. The patient's responses may be dissipated in activity between sessions and thus lost for therapeutic scrutiny. Or the patient may try to prolong the session in order to respond, leading to an uncomfortable and unnecessary tension. In general, the therapist should try to limit the number of interpretations within a single session. Interpretations have the most impact when they are carefully spaced. A single interpretation or connected series of partial interpretations in one session is ideal, since this has the greatest impact and allows adequate time to explore implications and the patient's responses.

Interpretations of important issues should ideally not be made prior to long breaks in the treatment, such as before vacations or other extended interruptions. In analysis, after a day-to-day rhythm to the work develops, many analysts prefer not to make interpretations that lead into important new areas during the last session of the week, in order to avoid the dissipating and obscuring effect of the weekend break. In once-a-week therapy, the situation is obviously different. What is important, in every instance, is to consider the issue of timing, both within sessions and in relation to the time between sessions.

All interpretations have a certain painful quality to them in the sense that they reveal to the patient something the therapist knows about the patient, which the patient might have known about himself, were it not for his problems, internal resistances, infantile amnesia, and other factors. Often this general or nonspecific painful aspect compounds the painful specific content of the interpretation, which perhaps reveals some uncomfortable, embarrassing, or critical material about the patient. The therapist, in thinking about the timing of interpretations, should take into account how much "pain" the patient can take at any given time and still be able to use the understanding the interpretation is designed to provide. One should always try to judge the patient's reflective capacity in timing interpretations. Interpretations made when the patient seems distraught, frightened, depressed, or otherwise intensely involved in some feeling state are rarely as effective as the therapist would like. By the same token, the therapist must keep in mind that certain patients will use emotional upset or accentuation of the "painful" aspect of interpretations to ward off the making of interpretations or to defend against having to think about them. As the therapist becomes better acquainted with the patient, these issues will become clearer and a certain rhythm of interpretation, which differs among patients, will be established. Paying careful attention to the patient's associations following interpretations is the best guide in arriving at a sense of timing appropriate to the patient.

Thus far, the timing issues with respect to making interpretations have been general ones in the sense of being unrelated to specific content. An overriding technical precept with regard to the content of interpretations and their timing concerns how far away from the patient's conscious awareness this content is. Freud (1913) put it thusly: "one must be careful not to give a patient the solution of a symptom or the translation of a wish until he is already so close to it that he has only one short step more to make in order to get hold of the explanation for himself" (S.E., p. 140). This general principle of interpretation plays a role in determining both when to interpret and how far to go in revealing new information to the patient. Care should be taken not to get too far ahead of the patient for many reasons. First, the therapist must know where the patient's conscious awareness of a particular issue ends. Interpretations should push the patient's knowledge ahead only a bit further in order not to meet with intense resistance, which will render the new information useless or provoke new defensive measures. Second, interpretations that go "too deep," are "too surprising," or are "incredibly perceptive" interfere with the therapeutic alliance in that they do not contain any contribution from the patient. They foster a sense of the therapist as a special commentator on the patient's hidden life, rather than as a collaborator with the patient in the understanding of his problems. Many patients feel unsafe with therapists who know "too much." Their anxieties and resistance intensify. Interpretations that go "too deep" are often felt to be unempathic by patients. They experience the therapist as not in touch with where they are. Third, interpretations that go too deep and are too surprising foster a view of the therapist as magical, wizardlike, and special. This may lead to a certain kind of fearful idealization of the therapist, which is difficult to interpret within the transference because the therapist, by his poorly timed interpretations, fosters such distortions. Last, the patient is deprived of any sense of self-discovery. The sense of participating in new discoveries about himself helps the patient in many ways. It fosters self-analytic work after the formal treatment ends. It counteracts undue dependence on the therapist in trying to understand problems. It increases self-esteem in the sense of being active in helping oneself, in mastering emotional difficulties. Thus, before an interpretation is made, the therapist should determine what the patient knows about a particular issue, what is the next bit of information in a logical, sequential uncovering of the unconscious aspects of this issue, what resistances to uncovering can be expected, what frame of mind the patient is in with respect to being able to observe, and to what extent the new information is "close at hand" or totally unexpected.

Another general principle of interpretation that concerns timing is the idea of interpreting material when it has become a resistance. There are many versions of this principle. "Only interpret the transference when it becomes a resistance." "Interpret resistance before content." "Never bypass a resistance." What these ideas have in common is their reference to resistance as a signal about when to intervene as well as what to address. Freud (1912a) laid down an early precursor of this principle in his advice that the interpretive process should begin when something interferes with the process of free association. Resistance usually increases the tension between patient and therapist and, in that sense, often prompts some kind of action from the therapist in order to reestablish a more comfortable feeling in the work. Often this process is largely unconscious, yet it contributes to the timing of interpretations. At a conscious level, a steady focus on the resistant aspects of what the patient is saying, feeling, and doing is a useful guide in deciding when to interpret. When resistance seems to predominate, interpretive intervention is usually called for. Resistance indicates that the patient feels threatened by the material at hand. The reasons for being fearful must be explored before or in conjunction with the new material being advanced. To bypass resistance is almost always a mistake. Yet it is worth mentioning that there are times in treatment when interpretations are made in response to issues other than emerging resistances. Early transference interpretations (Chapter 5) and early interpretations that foster the therapeutic alliance (Chapter 3) have already been described. The therapist should use resistance as a signal to guide the timing and content of interpretation. He need not, however, restrict his interpretations to instances in which resistance predominates.

Just as an increase in resistance can signal the need for interpretive intervention, so can the occurrence of certain other familiar therapeutic "events," many of which have already been described as usually requiring immediate attention leading to interpretation. Slips of the tongue, acting out, the early reports of dreams, boundary disturbances of various kinds, threats to the continuation of the treatment, and other "special" therapeutic developments are examples of other signals to intervene. Consideration given to the possible effects of not interpreting in the face of such signals usually indicates rather clearly whether an interpretation is called for. However, no "signals" are absolute in the sense of making interpretations imperative. In fact, because interpretations have meaning to patients that are unrelated to their content (i.e., interpretations as gifts, as signs of interest or love, as proof of the patient's influence over the therapist, as attacks), patients may unconsciously try to induce interpretations by "signals," which they have learned usually lead to interventions by the therapist. Whenever the therapist feels forced to interpret, a search for such a hidden motivation is warranted.

Conclusion

The interpretive process is the central therapeutic activity of the therapist. Interpretation involves skills the therapist gradually learns during his training and in his subsequent work with patients. Interpreting is governed by the principles outlined in this book. Such principles and their implementation obviously depend upon a correct understanding of the patient and of the therapeutic process. This book has focused specifically on the interpretive process itself in the belief that certain formal guidelines, rules, and principles help make interpretation a skill or technique that can be learned, improved upon, and studied. It is a technique that is often relatively ignored in psychotherapy training programs, leading to clumsy, ineffective, and counterproductive clinical work.

As the principles of interpretation are mastered, they gradually become preconscious activities of the therapist. The therapist adapts his interpretive approach to each patient's needs. In sound clinical work, in which the therapist and patient are empathically attuned, therapeutic dialogue will develop naturally and will vary over time in many of its aspects. The principles of interpretation described here will act as guidelines. They will serve as preconscious signals, as organizing matrices, as first approximations, as points of reference. The patient and therapist will talk to each other in a way that is their own personal creation and unique to their situation. When the therapist feels restricted by the underlying principles of interpretation, it is usually because he misunderstands them or is defensively clinging to them.

They are designed to help the therapist make the most useful contributions possible to the therapeutic work. As a technique, they must be learned and mastered. As in art, technical soundness allows for freedom of expression and for powerful communication. Without technique, little is said and less is heard.

Suggested Readings

Freud, S. (1914). Remembering, repeating and working-through. *Standard Edition* 12:147–156.

> This paper is included here because it contains the first appearance of the concept of working through. It is, in fact, a wide-ranging paper, which touches on aspects of transference, resistance, the repetition compulsion, and other important psychoanalytic concepts.

Greenson, R. R. (1965a). The problem of working through. In *Drive, Affects, Behavior*. Ed. M. Schur. New York: International Universities Press.

> The author surveys the literature on working through and offers abundant clinical material to illustrate problems in this area of therapeutic work. He views working through as those aspects of the treatment that make insight effective in terms of leading to significant and lasting changes in the patient. Insight precedes working through. Analytic work on those resistances that block insight is the analytic work proper. "The analysis of those resistances which keep insight from leading to change is the work of working through" (p. 282). The author emphasizes the importance of an intact working alliance for working through.

Karush, A. (1967). Working through. *Psychoanalytic Quarterly* 30:497–531.

> This is a particularly clear overview of the various elements of the therapeutic process subsumed under the term working through. After a thoughtful historical review of the concept, Karush describes working through in several contexts, offering clinical illustrations to support his ideas. He especially emphasizes the analyst's active role in encouraging working through within an interpretive context and underlines the importance of the analyst as an object for identification, while recognizing the dangers of misusing this mode of facilitating working through.

Loewald, H. W. (1960). On the therapeutic action of psycho-
analysis. *International Journal of Psycho-Analysis* 41:16–33.

> This classic contribution to the understanding of how analytic
> treatment brings about change in the patient serves as a useful
> backdrop for thinking about the therapeutic action of interpreta-
> tions. It emphasizes the synergism between the function of inter-
> pretation and the important new kind of object relationship the
> therapist offers the patient by virtue of his interest in and under-
> standing of unconscious processes within the patient, allowing
> for new integration and psychic reorganization. The author makes
> important contributions to our understanding of neutrality and
> objectivity in the therapist as they relate to his also being a
> potentially new object for the patient. Loewald's formulations
> help make it clear how the therapist's main activity of interpret-
> ing is supported and facilitated in its therapeutic effect by the
> therapeutic relationship without the latter becoming a purpose-
> fully contrived or manipulated therapeutic force.

Schafer, R. (1976). *A New Language for Psychoanalysis*. New
Haven: Yale University Press.

> This work is the author's attempt to reformulate psychoanalytic
> ideas in a language of actions rather than mental substantives,
> forces, structures, instincts, and the like. It is a clinical language
> close to the patient's experience. As such, it is also a language of
> interpretation, devoid of jargon, technical terms, and intellectual-
> ization. It is in this regard that this work is useful in connection
> with the principles of interpretation. Although the beginner and
> non-psychoanalyst will find much of the author's writing some-
> what difficult, it is worth careful study because it is helpful in
> translating the theoretical into the clinical, regardless of whether
> Schafer's new language adequately replaces our current psycho-
> analytic theoretical way of saying things. In many ways, "action
> language" has always been the preferred language of interpre-
> tation.

References

Adler, G. (1979). The myth of the alliance with borderline patients. *American Journal of Psychiatry* 136:642-645.

Altman, L. L. (1969). *The Dream in Psychoanalysis*. New York: International Universities Press.

Arlow, J. A. (1961). Silence and the theory of technique. *Journal of the American Psychoanalytic Association* 9:44-55.

―――― (1979). The genesis of interpretation. *Journal of the American Psychoanalytic Association Suppl.* 27:193-206.

Asch, S. S. (1976). Varieties of negative therapeutic reaction and problems of technique. *Journal of the American Psychoanalytic Association* 24:383-409.

Bird, B. (1972). Notes on transference: Universal phenomenon and hardest part of analysis. *Journal of the American Psychoanalytic Association* 20:267-301.

Brenner, C. (1979). Working alliance, therapeutic alliance, and transference. *Journal of the American Psychoanalytic Association Suppl.* 27:137-158.

Breuer, J., and Freud, S. (1895). Studies on Hysteria. *Standard Edition* 2:255-305.

Curtis, H. C. (1979). The concept of therapeutic alliance: Implications for the "Widening Scope." *Journal of the American Psychoanalytic Association Suppl.* 27:159-192.

Daniels, R. S. (1969). Some early manifestations of transference. *Journal of the American Psychoanalytic Association* 17:995–1014.

Erikson, E. H. (1954). The dream specimen of psychoanalysis. *Journal of the American Psychoanalytic Association* 2:5–56.

Firestein, S. K. (1974). Termination of psychoanalysis of adults: A review of the literature. *Journal of the American Psychoanalytic Association* 22:873–894.

Freud, A. (1968). Acting Out. *International Journal of Psycho-Analysis* 49:165–170.

Freud, S. (1900). The Interpretation of Dreams. *Standard Edition* 45:1–625.

—— (1901). The Psychopathology of Everyday Life. *Standard Edition* 6:53–105.

—— (1912a). The dynamics of transference. *Standard Edition* 12–99, 108.

—— (1912b). Recommendations to physicians practicing psychoanalysis. *Standard Edition* 12:111–120.

—— (1913). On beginning the treatment. *Standard Edition* 12:123–144.

—— (1914). Remembering, repeating and working-through. *Standard Edition* 12:147–156.

—— (1923). The Ego and the Id. *Standard Edition* 19:3–66.

—— (1937). Analysis terminable and interminable. *Standard Edition* 23:216–253.

Gill, M. M. (1979). The analysis of the transference. *Journal of the American Psychoanalytic Association Suppl.* 27:263–289.

Gill, M. M., and Muslin, H. L. (1976). Early interpretation of transference. *Journal of the American Psychoanalytic Association* 24:779–794.

Greenacre, P. (1954). The role of transference. *Journal of the American Psychoanalytic Association* 2:671–684.

Greenson, R. R. (1961). On the silence and sounds of the analytic hour. *Journal of the American Psychoanalytic Association* 9:79–84.

—— (1965a). The problem of working through. In *Drive, Affects, Behavior*. Ed. M. Schur. New York: International Universities Press.

—— (1965b). The working alliance and the transference neurosis. *Psychoanalytic Quarterly* 23:155–181.

────── (1967). *The Technique and Practice of Psychoanalysis.* New York: International Universities Press.

────── (1970). The exceptional position of the dream in psychoanalytic practice. *Psychoanalytic Quarterly* 39:519–549.

Greenson, R. R., and Wexler, M. (1969). The non-transference relationship in the psychoanalytic situation. *International Journal of Psycho-Analysis* 50:27–39.

Karush, A. (1967). Working through. *Psychoanalytic Quarterly* 36:497–531.

Kernberg, O. (1965). Notes on countertransference. *Journal of the American Psychoanalytic Association* 13:38–56.

────── (1976). Technical considerations in the treatment of borderline personality organization. *Journal of the American Psychoanalytic Association* 24:795–829.

Langs, R. (1975a). The patient's unconscious perception of the therapist's errors. In *Tactics and Techniques in Psychoanalytic Therapy.* Vol. II. *Countertransference.* Ed. P. Giovacchini. pp. 239–250. New York: Jason Aronson.

────── (1975b). The therapeutic relationship and deviations in technique. *International Journal of Psychoanalytic Psychotherapy* 4:106–141.

────── (1975c). Therapeutic misalliances. *International Journal of Psychoanalytic Psychotherapy* 4:77–105.

────── (1976). *The Bipersonal Field.* New York: Jason Aronson.

Loewald, H. W. (1960). On the therapeutic action of psychoanalysis. *International Journal of Psycho-Analysis* 41:16–33.

Loewenstein, R. M. (1956). Some remarks on the role of speech in psychoanalytic technique. *International Journal of Psycho-Analysis* 37:460–468.

────── (1963). Some considerations of free association. *Journal of the American Psychoanalytic Association* 11:451–473.

Macalpine, I. (1950). The development of the transference. *Psychoanalytic Quarterly* 19:501–539.

MacKinnon, R. A., and Michels, Robert. (1971). *The Psychiatric Interview in Clinical Practice.* Philadelphia: W. B. Saunders Company.

Miller, I. (1965). On the return of symptoms in the terminal phase of psychoanalysis. *International Journal of Psycho-Analysis* 46:487–501.

Modell, A. H. (1976). "The holding environment" and the therapeutic action of psychoanalysis. *Journal of the American Psychoanalytic Association* 24:285–307.

Moore, B. E. (1968). Contribution to symposium on acting out. *International Journal of Psycho-Analysis* 49:182–184.

Olinick, S. L. (1964). The negative therapeutic reaction. *International Journal of Psycho-Analysis* 45:540–548.

Orr, D. W. (1954). Transference and countertransference: A historical survey. *Journal of the American Psychoanalytic Association* 2:621–670.

Rangell, L. (1968). A point of view on acting out. *International Journal of Psycho-Analysis* 49:195–201.

Reich, A. (1960). Further remarks on countertransference. *International Journal of Psycho-Analysis* 41:389–395.

Reich, W. (1949). *Character Analysis*. New York: Noonday Press.

Schafer, R. (1968). The mechanisms of defence. *International Journal of Psycho-Analysis* 49:49–62.

—— (1973a). The idea of resistance. *International Journal of Psycho-Analysis* 54:259–285.

—— (1973b). The termination of brief psychoanalytic psychotherapy. *International Journal of Psychoanalytic Psychotherapy* 2:135–148.

—— (1976). *A New Language for Psychoanalysis*. New Haven: Yale University Press.

—— (1982). Problems of technique in character analysis. *Bulletin of the Association for Psychoanalytic Medicine* 21:91–99.

Sterba, R. F. (1934). The fate of the ego in analytic therapy. *International Journal of Psycho-Analysis* 15:117–126.

Stone, L. (1961). *The Psychoanalytic Situation*. New York: International Universities Press.

—— (1973). On resistance to the psychoanalytic process. *Psychoanalysis and Contemporary Science* 2:42–73.

Tower, L. E. (1956). Countertransference. *Journal of the American Psychoanalytic Association* 4:224–256.

Waelder, R. (1930). The principle of multiple function. *Psychoanalytic Quarterly*, 5:45–62.

Winnicott, D. W. (1949). Hate in the counter-transference. *International Journal of Psycho-Analysis* 30:69–74.

Zetzel, E. R. (1956). Current concepts of transference. *International Journal of Psycho-Analysis* 37:369–376.

Index